WRITERS AND CRITICS

||||||||||||||||||||||||||||||

Chief Editors

A. NORMAN JEFFARES
R. L. C. LORIMER

SHAKESPEARE

II

1587-1598

GARETH LLOYD EVANS

OLIVER AND BOYD

EDINBURGH

OLIVER AND BOYD LTD

Tweeddale Court
14 High Street,
Edinburgh EH1 1YL

05 002150 8 Hardback
05 002149 4 Paperback

Printed in Great Britain for Oliver and Boyd Ltd
by T. and A. Constable Ltd, Edinburgh

PREFACE

The first volume (Shakespeare I 1564-1592) of this series on Shakespeare's life and work concerned itself with his beginnings at Stratford and with those plays of his apprentice period. The present volume discusses the theatre context of his early days in London, and the plays in which he began to acquire, and display mastery over, his craft and art. The plan of the book follows that laid down in the first volume, and which will be the basis for the future volumes in the series. Where possible the plays are discussed in chronological order, to reveal the expansion of Shakespeare's vision, and his technical skill. The emphasis is on the reality of the plays in the theatre; there is, therefore, frequent reference to performances and to the experience we have of them in the auditorium.

It is hoped that the method adopted here will give a cohesive picture of the growth of a dramatist's genius, and that the student and the theatre-goer will both find that their interests have been catered for.

The notes to each chapter incorporate a specific bibliography for each volume. A larger and more comprehensive bibliography is planned for a later volume. In all quotations for the plays the original spelling and punctuation are left substantially unmodernised. The texts used for each play are as follows; *King John*, *Henry V*, *The Merry Wives of Windsor*—the First Folio. *Richard II*—First Folio and First Quarto; *1 Henry IV*—First Quarto, with some reference to the First Folio. *2 Henry IV*—First Quarto, with reference to the First Folio. *Romeo and Juliet*—Quarto, with reference to the First Folio. *The Merchant of Venice*—First Folio. The following alterations have been made silently: short "s" is used for long "s". "i/j", "u/v" and "w/vv" are normalised. Common Elizabethan abbreviations like y^r for "your" and n for "nn" are expanded in full, as are ampersands.

The academic debts of this book are implicit in the text and are acknowledged in the bibliographical references. Considering, however, the extent of the illumination which I have gained from innumerable performances, from conversations with players, directors and designers, it is impossible to acknowledge gratitude in detail. If the beneficial effects of so much, so dispersed and so enlivening an education are not apparent in the book, the fault is mine.

GARETH LLOYD EVANS

Stratford-upon-Avon 1969

CONTENTS

I

SHAKESPEARE IN LONDON
1587-1594

The few extant facts about Shakespeare's working life in the period 1587 to 1594 suggest, very strongly, that he was also consolidating himself in respects other than as a creative dramatist. It cannot be overemphasised that the theatre conditions in which he worked gave ample scope to the development, not only of dramatic talents, but also (for the shrewd and thrifty) opportunity for financial gain. Despite all the vicissitudes to which the acting companies and commercial theatres were subjected, by plague, fierce rivalry, censorship, and the unsympathetic ministrations of the authorities, there were gains to be made. Speculators like Henslowe were not slow to realise that money could be made out of drama. It is not difficult to accept, with the facts at our disposal, that Shakespeare was no less shrewd and farsighted in the handling of his business affairs than some of his fellows. The theatre world was a totality and made it natural for him to try and exploit every quality at his disposal—genius as a writer, mere talent as an actor, and native shrewdness as a speculator and shareholder. By 1599 he had acted with the Lord Chamberlain's men at Greenwich Palace, had shared in a payment of twenty pounds (a substantial sum) for plays performed before the Queen, and had received the satisfaction of hearing about the grant of a coat of arms to his father. By this date he had appeared regularly with the Lord Chamberlain's company and had purchased two cottages, two barns, and New Place. A further testimony to his growing prosperity was his receipt of begging letters and business proposals: in 1598 Richard Quiney asked for a loan of forty pounds and, in the same year, Quiney's father suggested a business proposal. Financial speculation which is suggested by these facts was given a sound basis by Shakespeare's acquisition of shares in the Globe Theatre in 1599. The relative economic stability which his connexion with this theatre gave him seems to have remained with him for the rest of his life—Shakespeare, throughout the greater part of his working career, was a Globe man. These hints of an advance towards affluence may suggest thrift but need not be equated with parsimony. True to the traditions of his profession Shakespeare does not seem to have put down roots in these early years in London, though he may well have been preparing for a later, more settled existence.[1]

In 1597 he was living in St Helen's Bishopsgate and, two years later, in the Clink on Surrey Bankside. Several examples of non-payment of tax occur in this period—November 1597 and 1598 and in October 1599—each one signified and dignified in a sombre Latin which gives us the poet's place of residence:

> Willelmus Shakespeare in parochia sancte Helene in Warda predicta debet xiijs iiijd.[2]

Within the smaller, less complicated environment of Stratford in the 1570s and 1580s and with the evidence available about his family and its connexions, speculation about him has a firm footing. In London, much of him, apart from the superb textures of his mind, is lost. In Stratford he may have stood out as a prodigy or even a freak; in London, at least until the mid-nineties, he was no more than one among a number of bright men. He belonged to a profession whose very nature can explain the lack of documentation about him and, indeed, about many of his fellows; the world of theatre is too unsettled to allow of the careful accretion of the bits and pieces of existence. It was a profession whose status was a contradiction—it made for unsettlement when, one hour, a Queen would greet and applaud and, the next, plague and city ordinances sent the players scuttling away like vagabonds. Shakespeare knew the unease of such a life and states it wryly: "The best in this kind are but shadows; and the worst are no worse, if imagination amend them." At Christmas 1594 he performed before the Queen at Greenwich; in 1597 his profession was described thus in a letter from the Lord Mayor and City Aldermen to the Privy Council:

> they are a special cause of corrupting their youth, containing nothing but unchaste matters, lascivious devices, shifts of cozenage, and other lewd and ungodly practices . . .[3]

Any attempt to visualise Shakespeare in London must be made in the light of this contradictory environment. What we know of twentieth-century theatre cannot be of much help for the simple reason that the theatrical profession has now become respectable in its society, and the structure of its organisation has changed. The Elizabethan theatre had its stars as ours has; the scanty references to Burbage support this:

> Hee's gone & with him what a world are dead,
> Which he revived, to be revived soe.
> No more young Hamlett, ould Heironymoe.
> Kind Leer, the greved Moore, and more beside,
> That Lived in him, have now for ever dyde.[4]

It depended as much upon fortune as upon talent, as does our theatre. It threw to the surface, and to fame, a clutch of dramatists, as ours has done. Yet there are strong differences. Acting companies (certainly the famous ones) stayed together longer than do modern ones. This is not to say that there was no to-ing and fro-ing between different companies; there was, but the sense of continuing ensemble is stronger than the sense of continual change. The many vicissitudes to which companies were subjected perhaps aided the feeling of fellowship. The plague, of itself a frightful visitation, had an ironic meaning for the actors, by association:

> the cause of plagues is sinne, if you looke to it well: and the cause of sinne are playes: therefore the cause of plagues are playes.[5]

The ordinances of the city fathers often took advantage of the threat of plague to clamp down upon the unwanted players:

> The assembly of people to plays, bearbaiting, fencers and
> profane spectacles at *The Theatre* and *Curtain* and other like
> places to which do resort great multitudes of the basest
> sort of people and many infected with sores running on
> them being out of our jurisdiction and some whom we
> cannot discern by any diligence . . . [6]

It is possible to accept the authorities' concern without forgetting
that, almost invariably, a moral judgment was involved in the
practicalities. The preacher who equated plague with play had
an ally in authorities who could add to a reasoned statement, the
"advancement of incontinency", "ungodly confederacies", and
"God's wrath".

Men, therefore, in a profession where kit bags had to be packed
and horses saddled at a moment's notice, acquired a fellowship
which was hard to shake. In such a fellowship the creative writer
was of particular importance. In the modern theatre the impression
is often given that the dramatist is a necessary nuisance—the mot
of a modern director to the effect that the job of the playwright
is to create a masterpiece, leave it at the stage-door, and go home
and commit suicide is less bizarre than indicative of an attitude.
In the Elizabethan theatre no such implied creative apartheid
existed, and for quite practical reasons. Runs of plays were very
short by our standards—the playwright's alchemy was continually
needed. More than this, the intense rivalry between companies,
and the demands of touring, put a premium on the clever,
quick writer. If a company had a versatile and speedy writer, it
would be loath to let him go. In any case, there was always, for a
successful company, the possibility of a sudden royal command;
if the Queen demanded a new play for a visiting dignitary, she
must have one. There is no reason to dismiss the story concerning
the occasion for the writing of *The Merry Wives of Windsor*:

> This Comedy was written at her command, and by her
> direction, and she was eager to see it Acted, that she
> commanded it to be finished in fourteen days . . . [7]

Those critics who find it difficult to believe that a new play could
be written in this period of time neglect three things: one, the

working conditions of the Elizabethan theatre; two, the persuasive-ness of royal necessity to invention; and, three, the hurried nature of the play itself.

Shakespeare was totally involved in his theatre in a sense in which neither his critics nor his modern directors and adaptors can ever be. It is an arrogance to suppose that we can know more about the realisation of his plays upon the stage than he did. All we have more than he had are extraneous aids to titillate the palates of twentieth-century audiences—lighting, make-up, and the electronic and technological comforters to the unimaginative. Shakespeare knew his theatre in every aspect of its working. As a leading actor he eventually became a shareholder and, as such, had a decisive part to play in the employment of other actors, Again, as shareholder, he would have played an active part in the apprenticeship system for the training of boy-actors. As actor and playwright he would have known and experienced the incredibly comprehensive skills that were required for the art of dramatic communication, involving dance, song, rhetoric, fencing, movement. The training in rhetorical speaking, that many actors had experienced at grammar school, was continued in the theatre; the ability to sing and dance was naturally expected; skill in swordsmanship was demanded by the plays, and, ironically, by the peril in which actors lived.

The theatre took up most of Shakespeare's time; this is a self-evident fact which seems to elude those who cannot understand how he came to write so much. He was writing, moreover, in an atmosphere which was completely congenial, since he wrote for profit, for his fellows, and for eager audiences, but not for posterity, and critics. This meant that the nature of what we call his text was fluid. The close relationship with actors would often bring about chops and changes in what was first conceived by the playwright, to meet the wishes of temperament, intuition, or audience reaction. The "text" insofar as it is thought of as the single work of one mind was not sacrosanct, nor would Shake-speare have conceived of it as so being. The "authority" of the Shakespearean text which scholars now often appeal to and directors flout, lay then, and still lies, in a corporate wholeness.

This is not to make out a case for constant multiple authorship, with fingers of all kinds in the pie; it is, rather, to recognise that the individual creative writer, like Shakespeare, would naturally accept that the final act of creation came with stage-realisation and that the "text" was what was acted, not what was written down.

It has been noted that the conditions in London made it inevitable that, from time to time, Shakespeare would have had to prepare hurriedly to leave for a provincial tour. It is possible that some of these tours took him very near to the family he had left in Stratford. M. M. Reese[8] believes that he installed his family in a substantial house in Bishopsgate and that they lived there until the purchase of New Place in 1597. This cannot be supported, although it must be recorded that his two brothers, Edmund and Gilbert may have lived in London in the 1590s. In 1607 an Edmond Shakespeare, "A player", was buried at St Mary Overies in Southwark and in 1597 a Gilbert Shakespeare is recorded as a resident in St Bride parish. The care and shrewdness which even the scanty facts about Shakespeare's activities strongly suggest, lead one to conjecture that he would not have exposed his wife and young children to the hazards of London. It is an extraordinary fact that, during the time when he was fast building a reputation, his chosen profession was subject to the greatest difficulties. The theatres were closed from 1592 to 1594 because of plague; outbreaks of the disease, of varying intensity, were frequent in the 1590s. This situation argues for his leaving his family in Stratford and for a tremendous concentration of creative and theatrical activity in those relatively free periods from the plague.

Shakespeare's life in London was busy and adventurous, exciting and dangerous. The plays were shaped and moulded not in the satin quiet of speculation but in the garish noise of working life. Ivor Brown conjures the atmosphere well and reasonably:

> Obviously his mind ranged widely, but he was not a
> consistent and committed man with a clear-cut philosophy.
> Amid a life of such various activities, his thinking was
> quick, impulsive and intermittent. He was obviously no
> tenant of an ivory tower: we know that he lived beside his

work in the busiest parts of the town, at one time amid the closepacked squalor of the Southwark Bankside with its stews and bear-garden as well as its theatres. . . . As the pamphleteers so angrily complained, London was a noisy town of narrow, crowded streets and raucous street-cries. No doubt he treasured the tranquillity of Stratford when he returned there, but during most of his life he could do quite well without it. [9]

Yet it is one thing to attempt, however tentatively, to visualise the man in London, quite another to know the specific details of his life and work. The facts are few, and speculation and deduction is baulked by the fact that he spent his early time in London when the theatre world was one of bewildering activity—itself thinly documented. It is not easy for us to imagine the implications of the simple fact that the 1580s and 90s saw the beginning of commercial professional theatre in this country. We take the present theatre-pattern for granted. Its beginnings, however, may be dimly understood by comparing them with the growth of the cinema in the 1920s. The growth of a new and large organisation, with little precedent to guide it, is bound to present a picture made up of dross, gold, success, failure, envy, fellowship, affection, and rancour. The history of the early cinema and the Elizabethan theatre is largely a history of bewildering strife, ending in the survival of the fittest, the giants emerging from the trampled remains of lesser beings.

Up to 1588 the Queen's Men, with whom it is possible Shakespeare arrived in London, were in the ascendancy. This was largely due to the popularity of its star actor—the clown, Tarlton, who died in that year. He was, in Heywood's words:

In his time gracious with the Queen, his sovereign, and in the people's general applause. [10]

By 1598 the company was in swift decline and a heart-catching story of their condition is evoked in Henslowe's words that "they broke and went into the contrey to playe". They left for the provinces and little more was heard of them in London.

Another company (The Lord Admiral's) are identifiable as a group as early as 1585, but on the departure of the Queen's Men they rose to the top, very much on the talented shoulders of one of their major shareholders—Edward Alleyn, the tragedian, of whom Jonson wrote:

> How can so great example dye in me
> That, Allen, I should pause to publish thee? ...
> Wear this renowne. 'Tis just, that who did give
> To many Poets life, by one should live.[11]

The Admiral's Men's status was itself threatened by the rise of Lord Strange's Men in the early 1580s, but both companies seem to have concluded that a loose form of merger was preferable to mutual extinction. By 1588 there was a liaison in the matter of employment of actors and a joint use of plays. In 1594, however, Lord Derby (patron to Strange's Men) died, and the two companies separated. At this point most of the former Strange's Men formed a company under the patronage of Lord Hunsdon and became known as the Lord Chamberlain's Men. Their fame and popularity grew, largely due to the genius of Richard Burbage, and later, by his depictions of Shakespeare's major tragic heroes.

By 1594, therefore, the year that Shakespeare is known to have joined the Lord Chamberlain's, this company and the Admiral's Men, who were driven ruthlessly by their manager Henslowe, dominated the London theatre.

If Shakespeare arrived in London with the Queen's Men and, following their decay, remained in London, by what process did he become, five years later, a member of the Lord Chamberlain's?[12]

Two companies which never achieved the eminence of the Chamberlain's and Admiral's are the most likely to have harboured Shakespeare after the demise of the Queen's Men. These (Pembroke's and Sussex's Men) attempted to gain strength by a form of affiliation. Some plays and actors passed from one to another, and it is conceivable that Shakespeare spent a few short years in their employ. A play called Titus Andronicus and one called The Taming of A Shrew were transferred from Pembroke's to the growing Lord Chamberlain's.

By this date his writings had received the favourable mention of Nashe, the strictures of Greene, and the ecstatic praise of Chettle. He was becoming well and quickly known. In the close, sometimes tense, personal relationships of that theatre world he would have known, in varying degrees of intimacy, all the theatre men of his day—the high and the low. It is not without reason to believe that his closest friends were the two men who were to achieve, by association with him, a golden memorial—Hemminges and Condell. They were actors in the Chamberlain's company, were left rings in his will and performed, perhaps without realising the consequences, the inestimable service for mankind of collecting their colleague's plays for publication seven years after his death.

Although he was, in a very positive sense, a man of business, one is inclined to feel that Shakespeare's warmer feelings, his deeper acquaintances, were with the players than with the cash-gazing tycoons with whom he had to deal and by whom his career was governed. Shakespeare's plays, from first to last, always recognise the world of commodity, of practicality, but their timeless verity lies elsewhere. It has its source in his sensitive knowledge that behind commodity and daily practice there is a world elsewhere which the poet uncovers and the actor embodies. For Shakespeare it is the actor who, by nature as well as by temperament walks the boundaries between "what is" and "what seems", between illusion and reality, between now and eternity. To touch the pulse of Shakespeare's love of the actors one can begin, fancifully and emotionally, by equating, for example, the roll-call of his fellow actors in the Lord Chamberlain's with that other roll-call asked for by one of his most astute actor/characters—Henry v. The vibrant sense of fellowship, of a love governed by the sentiment that men have lived and died together, is strong.

The demands of working in the forging-house of the Eliza-bethan theatre were persistent and many, but Shakespeare's energies in the 1590s were not all used up by his profession. *Venus and Adonis* was published in 1593 and *The Rape of Lucrece* in 1594. There is disagreement about the period in which he wrote the sonnets,[13] but there can be little doubt that they were created during a time when he was getting more and more involved in his work as a dramatist. It should occasion less surprise that he was able to write the sonnets when he was so heavily involved in other work than that they should be of such supreme literary merit. Like many of his fellows Shakespeare did not confine himself to one artistic discipline—specialisation was the exception rather than the rule in Elizabethan England.

It is remarkable enough that, in the years following his arrival in London up to the time when he became a shareholder in the newly built Globe Theatre in 1599, Shakespeare should have written so much and acquired so much prominence. It is, however, when the diversity of his work is examined that the true force and versatility of his imagination is realised. From the time he became a member of the Lord Chamberlain's Company in 1594 to its establishment at the Globe five years later he wrote lyrical romance, tragic history, lyric tragedy, and realistic comedy. In these five years and in those modes he wrote, among others, *A Midsummer Night's Dream*, *Richard II*, *Romeo and Juliet*, and *The Merchant of Venice*. In the same years he created Bottom, Shylock, Hal, Hotspur, Falstaff, the Nurse, Juliet, Mercutio, Benedick, Beatrice, and Dogberry.

This diversity and fecundity is startling in its implications about the nature of his mind. In any other playwright signs of restlessness and strain would undoubtedly show. There is no strain, no unsuccessful experimentation of any consequence, to be seen in Shakespeare's work. Moreover, this period of wide activity is, in some senses, only a prologue to even more remarkable things.

The scope and diversity of his work makes it difficult, in the absence of much external evidence, to be certain about the chronology of composition.[14] It is one thing for critical taste and judgment to be able, say, to see the lyrical consanguinities between *Romeo and Juliet* and *A Midsummer Night's Dream*, but quite another to state with any confidence that one play is undoubtedly earlier or later than the other. The traces of Senecan elements in *Romeo and Juliet* might lead the scholar to decide upon an earlier date for it, but other factors have prompted other scholars to suggest dates at various points between 1591 and 1596, with a consensus of opinion now for 1595. This could make the play later than *A Midsummer Night's Dream* which is generally accepted to have been written about 1594, though it is tempting to see in the latter's immaculate construction a more mature and later craftsmanship.

King John, again, is, chronologically, a problem play. Former scholars have ascribed it to 1595, 1596, and 1597, but the latest authoritative theory is for 1591. These examples make it clear that the problems are insoluble and that there must come a point where critical sensibility and intuition begin to exercise their admittedly dangerous influences upon decisions about the order of writing. It may very well be the case, indeed, that Shakespeare was engaged in writing more than one play at the same time. It is not without credence for two reasons. Firstly, his obvious rise in prominence as a literary man would have put his services in great demand and, secondly, multiple creative activity is common rather than rare in the world of theatre.

Certainly a persistent search for material for playwriting is suggested by what we know of Shakespeare's reading in the early 1590s. He remained faithful to his indispensable Holinshed for *Richard II*, *Henry IV*, and *Henry V*, but he was obviously also well acquainted with contemporary material—with Marlowe's *Edward II*, the anonymous play, *Thomas of Woodstock*, and with John Stow's *Chronicles*, Elyot's *The Governour*, and Samuel Daniel's *Civil Wars*.

For his non-historical plays he ranged widely for inspiration. Either in the original or in translation he knew various Italian versions of the story in Bandello, da Poito and Salernitano, and he had close knowledge of Brooke's *The Tragicall history of Romeus and Juliet* published in 1562. For *The Merchant of Venice* he turned again to Italy—to Boccacio's *Decameron* and Fiorentino's *Il Pecorone*, but knew, as well, Gower's *Confessio Amantis* and kept a wary eye on Marlowe's *The Jew of Malta*.

No source has been discovered for *A Midsummer Night's Dream*, a fact which engenders sentimentalism in some commentators—a feeling of being in the presence of Shakespeare's very own work. Yet it shows evidence of outside influence. For this play he had memories of reading Chaucer, North's *Life of Theseus*, Ovid's *Metamorphoses* and Scot's *Discoverie of Witchcraft*, with a shrewd look at his contemporary rival's play (Greene's *James IV*).

These are some of the books that we know with some certainty that he read or consulted;[15] there must be others that have remained unrecorded for us. The proponents of the view that his was an untutored and intuitive genius should take pause in the face of this evidence of reading; further, those who find it difficult to believe that in the hurly-burly world of theatre there would not have been time for much reading should take warning of the evidence revealed by the publication of Dylan Thomas's letters. Poets of a strong lyrical cast, like Shakespeare, Thomas, and, indeed, Keats, often suffer the fantasy that for them reading is both impossible and unnecessary. We have, of course, no letters or diaries to prove the opposite in Shakespeare's case, but the mere quantity of books which we know he must have read alone suggests that he found time to feed his mind from the work of others.

We must conceive of this period of his life in London as one in which his intellectual muscles and imaginative responses were being stretched and flexed by constant and diverse exercise. The evidence of his plays suggests that he had still not found a complete individuality, though in *Henry IV* he stands poised upon it. His imagination and dramatic skills were exercised in several different directions, as if the sources of power were trying to find the perfect access. Whether he was consciously aware of it or not, it is possible to see that what was happening in the group of plays which express the diversity of activity, was a gradual advance towards a unity of style and a synthesising of the separate modes of tragedy, comedy and history; or, to put it differently, he was advancing from being the best exponent of certain popular modes towards a total and unique individuality.

2

HISTORY

1. *Richard II*

Two of Shakespeare's history plays written in close proximity[1] to one another share a strange status in the whole canon of plays devoted to the unfolding of the story of Kings, nobles, and common men with which he was concerned for a great part of his working life. Neither *Richard II* nor *King John* sits very easily in the complicated pattern which binds the other histories together. The former, through its protagonist's fate, is the source of all that, historically, happens in the history plays but, in itself, it seems cast in a different dramatic mould. Although it directly and starkly shows the actions of conspiracy, the cares of kingship and the melée of faction which generate the main themes of all the histories, it is not for these that we remember or admire this play. It is a sad and lonely play largely because its king is a sad and lonely figure.

It is well, however, to remember, yet again, the difference in effect of a Shakespeare play upon its own and a twentieth-century audience. In the case of *Richard II* there is a very large and demonstrable gap between its original and present impact. Its historical implications have far less force and interest for us than they had for the Elizabethans. The play was written soon after the beginning of 1596. On 7 Feb. 1601 it was revived and performed by the Lord Chamberlain's Men on the afternoon before Essex's abortive rebellion. The circumstances of the play would have immediately found a strong echo in the contemporary scene. On 10 February Augustine Phillips, one of the Lord Chamberlain's Men, was examined under oath about the performance. The record tells

the story and affirms the connexion between the play and
contemporary events:

> He sayeth that on Fryday last was sennyght or Thursday Sr
> Charles Percy Sr Josclyne Percy and the L. Montegle with
> some thre more spak to some of the players in the presence
> of thys examinate to have the play of the deposyng and
> kyllyng of Kyng Richard the second to be played on
> Saterday next promysyng to get them xls. more than
> their ordynary to play yt. Wher thys Examinate and hys
> fellowes were determyned to have played some other play,
> holding that play of Kyng Richard to be so old & so long
> out of use as that they shold have small or no Company
> at yt. But at their request this Examinate and his fellowes
> were content to play yt the Saterday and had their xls.
> more than their ordynary for yt and so played yt
> accordyngly.[2]

It must be emphasised that there is strong evidence that, even
before this time, the play had been regarded as a comment (a
dangerous one), on political matters, for the deposition scene was
omitted from the published quarto of 1597. Its inclusion would
have been likely to rouse the Queen's anger. Throughout her
reign she was conscious of an ever-present threat of deposition
and, as she grew older, her lack of an heir only served to increase
her sensitivity to plots and stratagems. She does not, however,
seem to have blamed the actors or the playwright for the use made
of the play as a piece of political propaganda.

Yet all this is whirled away in the winds of time, and although
the political elements in it are strong, they do not incite us in this
age. It is their effect upon this isolated king that excites the modern
audience.

Two sides of Richard are presented. Indeed, a measure of
Shakespeare's skill is the manner in which he makes them
compatible although they differ considerably in essentials.
Richard is off-stage for eighty lines in Act Two, scene one, for
the whole of Act Two, scene two and scene three (which is very
long) and also for scene four and Act Three, scene one. It is

within this gap that we are prepared to meet with a Richard who shows a different side to his character from the one shown us in Act One. There seems to have been a deliberate attempt by Shakespeare to put Richard in the worst possible light in the first act. He is incapable of listening to others' arguments; he seems unaware of the potential danger to his throne in his banishment of Bolingbroke; he is indecisive and rash in his actions; he is totally reckless in agreeing to the levying of taxes which not only will be resented but are to be collected by an unpopular favourite of his own. All these faults may be judged as indicative of weak kingship and Shakespeare is relentless in keeping them before our attention. Yet this weakness, mixed with haughty arrogance, is not the whole of the picture. Further flaws are revealed and these point less to kingly insufficiency than to personal viciousness. Richard's behaviour to the dying Gaunt is insensitive, then arrogant, then cruel. There is nothing of the later poet in the Richard who stabs Gaunt with short, wounding phrases:

Can sicke men play so nicely with their names?

[II. I. 84]

Should dying men flatter with those that live?

[II. I. 88]

I am in health, I breathe, and see thee ill.

[II. II. 92]

His mocking reply to York who catalogues the wrongs Richard has committed—Gloucester's death, Bolingbroke's banishment— is simply: "Why, uncle, what's the matter?" His final act, before disappearing for a time, is to seize, incontinently, Gaunt's land and goods. Shakespeare completes, unequivocally, a dark portrait.

In the interim, before his return, his kingdom has begun to fall to pieces—rebellion is rife, disaffection appears in every corner. It is beyond the bounds of credence that we should begin to feel any sympathy for a king whose character has been so plainly shown to us. Yet, it is within this gap of Richard's absence that we are prepared to change our attitude. Ironically, it is York (who is most aware of the mistakes that Richard has made) who leads us to a point where a revaluation of our attitude towards this king is possible. York, throughout the play, is a representative of the status quo; he is a man whose principles are founded on the acceptance of the rule of law and order. York introduces the main historical theme of the play and, indeed, states a basic theme of Shakespeare's histories. He says to Bolingbroke:

> Thou art a banisht man and here art come,
> Before the expiration of thy time,
> In braving armes against thy sovereigne.
>   [II. III. 110-12]

The implications are clear—rebellion is a sin and, in rebelling, even against such a king, Bolingbroke cannot be excused.

When we next see Richard, therefore, another dimension has been added to the background of his character. Personally condemnable as he is, Shakespeare has now put him inalienably in a position of moral right. He *is* annointed king. The other side of Richard, which we now begin to see, is one which creates a tension between our knowledge of him as person and as victim of an illegal rebellion. We may never forget the Richard whom we saw at the lists or at the death-bed of Gaunt, but our condemnation of him must now have conditions to it. Shakespeare does not pause to ease us into this new dimension—its implications are apparent in both the meaning and the manner of Richard's words at Berkeley:

> Deere earth I do salute thee with my hand,
> Though rebels wound thee with their horses hoofes:
> As a long parted mother with her childe
> Plays fondly with her teares and smiles in meeting,
> So weeping, smiling greete I thee my earth,
> And do thee favours with my royal hands.
>   [III. II. 6-11]

Here, for the first time, the poet speaks. From this point onwards he has to be judged on the exquisite composition of his words. We may remember the insufficient man but we are forced now to witness one who celebrates through words the realities of his kingship. Richard, through adversity, has moved from petulant man into beleaguered king. He has become aware of the awesome fact of kingship and though, when he speaks, he still involves his personal feelings in his words, it is largely the articulate symbol of majesty that we hear. He is both poem and poet.

His thoughts and feelings are almost entirely inward-looking; practically his whole preoccupation is with himself as the theme of his poetic speculations upon kingship. As the play advances these speculations move from the general to the particular. When he first realises the extent of the rebellion it is the sanctity of kingship that concerns him:

> Not all the water in the rough rude sea,
> Can wash the balme off from an annointed King,
> The breath of worldly men cannot depose,
> The deputy elected by the Lord.
>
> [III. II. 54-7]

The subsequent success of the rebellion causes him more and more to identify his own person with the attributes of kingship. The process begins when he is told of the deaths of Bushy, Bagot, and Green. He indulges in a superb paean of grief about the cares of kingship and the vulnerability of that condition—in the speech which begins: "No matter where; of comfort no man speake/ Let's talk of graves, of wormes, and Epitaphs". But here the word "king" and the personal "I" become one in the form of a begging question:

> I live with bread like you, feele want,
> Taste griefe, neede friends, subjected thus,
> How can you say to me, I am a King?
>
> [III. II. 175-7]

This process of identification is rich in implications within Richard's mind. In his new-found consciousness of himself he not only begins to make "King" and "I" one flesh, but adds Christ to the reckoning—the ultimate symbol of rejected kingship on earth. The slightest indication of treachery will push Richard into a Christ-like posture. Believing (wrongly) that Bushy, Bagot, and Green are traitors he cries:

> Three Judasses, each one thrice worse than Judas!
>   [III. II. 132]

His frequent iteration of the divine right of kingship has, for
him, an additional potency in his role of Christ:

> If we be not, shew us the hand of God
> That hath dismist us from our Stewardship.
>   [III. III. 77-8]

The words he is given to use to express his chosen identification
with Christ are explicit,

> Did they not sometime cry all hayle
> To me? so *Judas* did to *Christ* . . .
>   [IV. I. 170-1]

and in a superb display of self-dramatisation he plots the way
whereby the earthly kingdom is abandoned for the kingdom of
heaven:

> And my large kingdome for a little grave,
> A little little grave, an obscure grave.
>   [III. III. 153-4]

Towards the end his self-dramatising imagery reaches a climax
of grandeur. He pushes the drama of self that he has created to an
ultimate conclusion. Only he himself is able to denude himself
of the grave splendour that he has, by his imagination and words,
encrusted about him. Bolingbroke stands curiously powerless,
while this great actor/poet dominates the stage. At this point
Richard has achieved the maximum effect that his imagination
can gain. The poet has created his masterpiece:

> Now marke me how I will undoe my selfe:
> I give this heavie weight from off my head,
> And this unwieldie Scepter from my hand,
> The pride of kingly sway from out my heart:
> With mine owne teares I wash away my balme,
> With mine owne hands I give away my Crowne,
> With mine owne tongue deny my sacred state,

With mine owne breath release all duties rites:
All pompe and majestie I do forsweare.

[IV. I. 201-9]

Yet neither Shakespeare nor, through him, Richard, has
finished with our emotions. Having satisfied, with grief-stricken
hedonism, his own imagination, Richard still has a trump to
play. After stripping himself as person and king, becoming a
nothing, he abandons his verbal voyaging with Christ, and plays
upon the simple fact that he has now become nothing. Bolingbroke
can merely abide while Richard dominates and makes his final
assault upon the world. He acts out, in a scene of dazzling and, in
every sense, theatrical power, the meaning of what has happened
to him. He has hypnotised us with words and now he taunts
Bolingbroke with one single histrionic deed:

Good King, great King; and yet not greatly good:
And if my name be sterling, yet in England,
Let it commaund a mirour hither strayte,
That it may shew me what a face I have,
Since it is bankrupt of his Majestie.

[III. I. 261-5]

The mirror is obtained and Richard continues:

Was this the face that fac't so many follies,
And was at last out-fac't by Bullingbrook?
A brittle Glorie shineth in this face,
As brittle as the Glorie is the face.

[IV. I. 280-3]

It is left to the Bishop of Carlisle to utter the internal meaning
of the events that have led to this scene:

The woe's to come; the children yet unborne,
Shall feele this day as sharpe to them as thorne.

These lines restore the play to its larger historical meaning.
Richard has taken us, for a time, out of the historical process and

bent our minds towards his individual grief and deprivation. Yet the fuller meaning is clear. The curse has fallen upon England. From this point onwards Shakespeare uses Richard himself to stress the historical meaning of what has happened. Though we do not lose sight of the suffering man, we are aware always of the grief to come to a whole kingdom:

> And some will mourne in ashes, some cole blacke,
> For the deposing of a rightfull King.
>
> [V. I. 49-50]

While it may be claimed that, for the twentieth century, the emphasis on Richard supplies the greater dramatic potency, we must beware of underrating the broader historical meanings of this play. At many points the external equivalents of Richard's inner torments are affirmed. York, having berated Richard for his shortcomings, is no less severe on Bolingbroke for his rebellion. Even Bolingbroke himself cannot forbear to see the grandeur of majesty in Richard. He expresses himself in words which echo Richard's own elevation of himself into a god-figure:

> See, see, King Richard doth himselfe appeare,
> As doth the blushing discontented Sunne,
> From out the fierie portall of the east.
>
> [III. III. 62-4]

Shakespeare paints Richard in dark colours at the beginning of the play, but it must be noted that the crime of Bolingbroke, and its sinfulness, is far from ignored. It receives oblique but effective utterance in Bolingbroke's own words at the end of the play:

> Lords, I protest my soule is full of woe,
> That blood should sprinckle me to make me grow.
>
> [V. VI. 45-6]

The point where the inward-turning imagery of Richard and the outer meaning of the events meet at a flashpoint is in the scene where the crown goes to Bolingbroke. Nowhere is the

validity of Richard's status as annointed king more directly
stated. Bolingbroke is invited to "seize" the crown; it is held
before him and mused upon by Richard. Bolingbroke is unable
to take it, and lamely reminds Richard that he thought he had
been willing to resign it. At the very moment of obtaining the
crown of England Bolingbroke enters into that characteristic
guilty inertia of will which dominates his character as Henry IV.
It is achieved by Richard's demonstration not so much of personal
grief as of the awesome reality of usurpation.

Indeed a kind of inertia is also characteristic of the whole
opposition to Richard. The rebellion itself has nothing of the
direct and bloody activity of the wars of the roses or the later
rebellion which, in turn, was to threaten Bolingbroke's throne.
The first scene at the lists and the gage-throwing scene have a
curiously statuesque and merely ceremonial quality. No battle
is seen in the play. There is an air of apology about the whole
matter, and a strong sense of incipient guilt. Only in theoretical
terms is Bolingbroke shown as capable of being a stronger, better,
king than Richard—we are mainly led to assume that this will
be so. In fact Shakespeare does not go out of his way to prove
Bolingbroke's superiority—he remains no more than an illegal
alternative to a demonstrably weak monarch. The play is held
fast in an atmosphere of grief, doubt and guilt—it never asserts
in action that might will triumph over weakness.

Richard II is the source play out of which the later historical
themes take their material. It begins the curse that must be
expiated. Yet it must be emphasised that it is very different in
kind from the rest. It is deficient in action; its "demonstration"
of history is subservient to the emphasis on the protagonist;
certain scenes, as has been mentioned, seem conceived less towards
forwarding the action than to presenting ritual or symbolic
pictures. Although, for example, it may be said that the scene
at the lists serves the necessary purpose of introducing the plot
and revealing something of Richard, its construction and movement rigidly and mechanically imitate the actual formalities
of a medieval tourney, Shakespeare has leaned heavily and
slavishly on Holinshed:

When he heard what they had answered, he commanded
that they should be brought foorthwith before his presence,
to heare what they would say. Herewith an herald in the
king's name with lowd voice commanded the Dukes to
come before the king, either of them to shew his reason, or
else to make peace togithir without more delaie. When
they were come before the king and lords, the king spake
himselfe to them, willing them to agree, and make peace
togithir: 'for it is' (said he) 'the best waie ye can take.' The
duke of Norfolke with due reverence hereunto answered,
it could not be so brought to passe, his honor saved . . .[3]

The scene, on stage, unless produced carefully, becomes a slightly
ludicrous panoply of antiquated ritual, and its dramatic purpose
can easily be lost. A more extreme example of a scene which does
not take wing out of mere ritual is the gage scene. Modern
producers have been known to cut it, and it is difficult not to
sympathise with them. Its presence can be theoretically justified
by claiming that it shows how the act of rebellion brings with
it internal dissensions—rebellion doomed to self-destruction. In
theatrical terms, however, it is difficult to produce the scene
without inducing a comic response from the audience. The
repetitive throwing-down of gages by a circle of noble lords
irresistibly conjures up a kind of musical-chairs behaviour. Recent
productions have shown that this effect cannot be removed even
by concentrating production on creating great and elaborate
ceremonial. The difficulty arises from the fact that there is no
variety in the ceremonial ingredients of the scene; more important,
nothing in its verbal pattern can lure the mind away from its
mechanical superficiality of construction and movement. Once
again it is undigested Holinshed:

'I say' (quoth he) 'that he was *the* verie *cause* of his death';
and so he appealed him of treason, offering by throwing
downe his hood as a gage to proue it with his bodie. There
were twentie other lords also that threw downe their hoods,
as pledges to proue the like matter against the duke of
Aumarle.[4]

The garden scene is in a different category. It is a characteristic example of Shakespeare's method, in the early histories, of allegorising the meaning of historical event. The garden is England; the message is simple. All the plants in the garden must be kept in due order, what is weed must be destroyed, what grows in too much profusion must be pruned, what is weak must be tended. The result must be order and due proportion.

The scene has, on occasions, been cut on the grounds that it interrupts the action and is too obvious an image of England's condition. If the scene were merely that, to cut it might be justifiable. It performs, however, another and most important function. It is largely through this scene that the character of Richard's Queen is given some substance. Up to this point she has been a shadowy creature, faithful but neglected. In this scene the agony of being Queen is brought home in a far more telling way than in, for example, *Richard III*. In that play there is something unbelievable about the collection of weeping ex-consorts who hold a prolonged wake on their grief. Here, however, a pathetic individual tragedy is sharply outlined. It is a well-unified scene. The garden is, as it were, real, the gardeners are real, the Queen is real. Yet both garden and gardeners are also symbolic and the scene proceeds on two levels—the one direct, the other implicit. In the end neither level dominates, but they merge into one complete and unified effect clinched by the gardeners' inclusion of the Queen within the symbolic pattern of the garden:

> Here did she fall a teare, here in this place
> Ile set a bank of Rew, sowre hearb of grace,
> Rew even for ruth, heere shortly shall be seene,
> In the remembrance of a weeping Queene.
>   [III. IV. 104-7]

The presence of such scenes of ritual and symbolism only serve to intensify the distinctiveness of *Richard II* as a history play, but they are aided by other factors. The primal curse which falls for centuries upon England as a result of Bolingbroke's usurpation is shown, in its working out, as vicious and brutal.

In *Henry IV*, as he had done in *Henry VI* and *Richard III*, Shakespeare shows the active results of the curse, but all the ingredients of history as Shakespeare saw them—rebellion, usurpation, divine right, honour, duty, patriotism—are curiously abstract in this play. Gaunt's speech on England celebrates an abstraction; Bolingbroke's rebellion stands back, as it were, from the forefront of the action—a cypher of disaffection rather than the thing itself; the jealousy of nobles is not shown in fierce stark brutality, but as a formal testy ritual; the realities of usurpation are talked about rather than shown in action. The play's motto might well be, in Aumerle's words: "No, good my lord; lets fight with gentle words." There is a withdrawal from the active facts of historical events. It is as if the whole play is a series of arranged tableaux illustrating, but not embodying, the great and abiding themes which are developed in the other histories.

What, more than anything, distinguishes this play and gives it the status of a lyrical peom is the language. A. C. Sprague[5] has truly written: "On Richard's lips the poetry of the young Shakespeare seems wholly natural". The important words are "young" and "poetry". The play is shaped on the same velvet anvil that created the sonnets, *Venus and Adonis* and *Romeo and Juliet*. The result is a rhythmical celebration of, and rumination on, action—not action itself. Indeed any movement towards action is stifled by the overwhelming interference of lyrical speech. It is noticeable how often Richard begins speeches with words which, as it were, announce a speech which will be of superb lyrical quality:

> Draw near,
> And list what with our council we have done.
> Mine eare is open, and my hart prepard.
> [III. II. 93]
>
> Lets talke of graves, of wormes, and Epitaphs.
> [III. II. 145]
>
> Now marke me how I will undoe my selfe.
> [IV. I. 201]

Richard's lyrical passages attain the condition of music. It is as if he makes a pathetic substitution for an order which his kingdom is losing by ordering his own thoughts and feelings in a musical pattern. In the end he finds that this is not enough. He hears music outside his cell and says:

> . . . Musicke do I heare;
> Ha, ha, keepe time; how sowre sweete musicke is,
> When Time is broke, and no proportion kept.
> [v. v. 41]

It plays on, but only reminds him of his approaching end. He shouts:

> This Musicke maddes me, let it sound no more.
> [v. v. 61]

but, at the last, with a curious indication of self-knowledge, he relents:

> Yet, blessing on his heart that gives it me,
> For t'is a signe of love; and love to *Richard*
> Is a strange Brooch in this al-hating world.
> [v. v. 64-6]

The music he has created through his words has been not only an attempt to hold fast to an order, a pattern, but an obbligato to his own love of himself. The tragedy of Richard II is that of the poet who, taking himself as his subject and theme, has fallen in love with what he has created. He has no qualifications whatsoever for the kind of kingship demanded by the abstractions of tradition and the actualities of political life, except for one thing—a sense of the superb grandeur of kingship. His tragedy, personally as it is expressed, has a certain irony in it. Like a poet, he knows and can communicate the truth of his own experience; unlike a poet he has been called upon, as king, to be and to do more than this. He is completely unequal to the task of being both poet and monarch.

B

2. *King John*

For thematic reasons it is difficult to equate this play with the
main historical series; moreover, doubts about its date of composition tend to isolate it from the grand design. There is no
quarto version and there is a considerable body of opinion which
claims that the folio text comes from Shakespeare's so-called
foul-papers. If this is so then it means that we are face to face with
a very early draft of the writing. The date of composition is
unknown, although a consensus puts it prior to *Richard II*.
Internal evidence presents the customary difficulties of weighing
possibility against instinct. *Richard II*, by reason of its lyrical
power and the strength of characterisation of the protagonist,
would seem to be a later play; on the other hand there are scenes
in *King John* which display a mastery of dramatic and theatrical
technique which seem superior to the other play. A prevalent
general view that it was written about 1594 has been strongly
challenged by E. A. J. Honigmann. [6] He bases his arguments upon
the relationship between this play and another—*The Troublesome
Rayne of King Johne of England*, published in two separate quartos
in 1591. Previously it had been broadly accepted that Shakespeare's
play was a rewriting of *The Troublesome Rayne* which, itself, was
an anonymous version of the story. Honigmann argues that, on
the contrary, *The Troublesone Rayne* is a bad quarto of Shakespeare's
own play.

It is true that there is much in the broad design of the two plays
which can be compared—the events chosen are similar, the time-
period covered is the same. There is, too, a singular and significant
omission in both plays—the signing of Magna Carta. It would be
folly, however, to conclude too much from these similarities,
since there is one vital and distinctive difference between them.
The Troublesome Rayne is palpably anti-Catholic; Shakespeare's
play, typically, does not definitely commit itself to siding with
any religious point of view. This fact, admittedly, is no reason
for concluding that Shakespeare is not one and the same author
of both plays, since he may have decided to tone down in one
version what amounted to anti-Catholicism in the other. The

question of the true relationship between the two plays rests. Suffice is it to say that, of the two versions, *King John* is immeasurably the better dramatic piece.

It stands apart from the other histories for two particular reasons. First, although the status of kingship—

> What earthie name to Interrogatories
> Can tak the free breath of a sacred King?
> [III. I. 147-8]

—is part of the groundswell of the play, it is not a dominant part. Second, although the fate of England is obviously involved in the action, it is not presented against the direct or implied background of the pattern of history, as it is in the other historical plays. The nature of the Bastard's character reinforces the difference from the other histories. The nature of this new kind of experience remains to be discussed, but its presence may be said briefly to affect our acceptance of the whole story and of the historical issues behind the plot.

It is difficult to account for its comparative neglect by theatrical history. It gives the director much scope for diversity of action, set and pace; its characters, both male and female, are, in several cases, strongly written. At least three of them (Constance, Blanche, and the Bastard) ought to prove irresistible to the acting profession. Yet, when it appears in the repertory of any theatre, it seems surprising that it should be there. Perhaps there is an irremovable psychological blockage to its acceptance by audiences. King John is the Demon King, after all, of our island story. His reputation as predator of the people's rights has given him a quasi-mythological status as the one really obvious tyrant that English history has produced—he is almost bad enough, in the popular imagination, to be a foreigner! Richard IIIrd is attractive in his villainy, but King John is beyond the pale. It is not without point to recall that one of the most successful modern interpretations (Robert Helpmann's at Stratford in 1948) was described by *Punch* as looking like "an emaciated King of Diamonds".

The dominant theme of the play has five aspects to it—each one announced and developed by different characters. The nub is the concept of right and succession, and its very different interpretations by different people. King John stands for sovereign right in terms of kingly rule, and Philip, thematically, is in the same camp. The second is the Bastard's claim to be recognised, to be given an identity. The third is the conception of right as seen and promulgated by the representative of the Holy See— Pandulph. The fourth is the strident, emotionally conceived and expressed sense of right in Constance. The fifth is the actual matter of the claims to the throne which are made on his behalf by the pathetic figure of Arthur.

The persistent and all-enveloping theme is announced at the very beginning of the play with Chatillon's statement that Philip of France's claims on behalf of John's nephew are sound. The atmosphere which is generated by the exchanges which follow pervades the whole action—it may be described as one of bickering and reasonless conceit. The theme has certain points of great emphasis, particularly in the actual physical confrontations between the contending parties. A superficial view of its treatment might conclude that its appearance is of the same nature as that of the *Henry VI* plays. At first glance it looks like the relentless pride and empty egotism which characterises the warring nobility in those plays. Yet, in fact, there is a subtle difference. There is a much stronger quality of implied condemnation of the bickering feuds than in the earlier plays. This condemnation eventually comes to the surface as a kind of mockery of the various assertions of right, might, and succession. The way that John, for example, is depicted, contains, at times, all the blimpery of a world war one General asserting claims to pieces of land that a million men will die for:

> Be thou as lightning in the eies of France,
> For ere thou canst report, I will be there:
> The thunder of my Cannon shall be heard.
>
> [I. I. 24-5]

The protestations of Arthur's supporters ring a little artificially. They protest, too much, their disinterestedness in the affair, and condemn themselves out of their own mouths with a holier-than-thou emphasis which makes us suspicious:

> Upon thy cheeke lay I this zelous kisse
> As seale to this indenture of my love:
> That to my home I will no more returne
> Till *Angiers* and the right thou hast in France
>
> .   .   .
>
> [II. I. 19-22]
>
> Salute thee for her King; till then faire boy,
> Will I not thinke of home, but follow Armes.
> [II. I. 30-1]

Again, King Philip's remark to John:

> *England* we love; and for that *Englands* sake,
> With burden of our armor heere we sweat
> [II. I. 91-2]

is as ironic in effect (though, on this occasion, perhaps unconsciously) as Henry v's celebrated remark to Kate that he loves France so much that he will not part with a yard of it.

If there were any doubt that Shakespeare's intention was to make these contestants condemn themselves, Act Two, scene one should remove them. The bickering which, for a time, is carried on in blustering rhetoric, suddenly becomes personal; the scene is reduced to the proportions of a petty family quarrel:

> K. JOHN: Alack, thou dost usurpe authoritie.
> K. PHILIP: Excuse it is to beat usurping downe.
> ELEANOR: Who is it thou dost call usurper *France*?
> CONSTANCE: Let me make answer: thy usurping sonne.
> [II. I. 118-21]

The rhetoric eventually returns but, this time, the contestants are ridiculed, in effect, by the reluctance of the people of Angiers to open their gates to either force. The play is pushed very near to the comic frontier in the episode where rival kings bombast their pride, right and might, and are coolly told that neither of them adds up to anything unless they can prove the contrary.

The sense of the ridiculous is increased by the interjections of the
Bastard in these noisy announcements and threats made by each
side:

> O, tremble: for you hear the Lyon rore.
>
> [II. I. 294]

The roar is, in fact, completely ineffectual.

The Bastard's presence governs one part of our reactions to
these events; it is through him that we are really convinced of
the bombastic pointlessness of it all. It is, however, the unwitting
cause of all the bombast who governs another part of our reactions—
Arthur, John's nephew. In the long scene of direct confrontation
at Angiers, he is present, an almost silent witness of events he
has unwittingly set in motion by existing. He is almost silent,
except that he utters two sentences—"I do beseech you, madam,
be content" and, pertinently:

> I would that I were laid low in my grave,
> I am not worth this coyle that's made for me.
>
> [II. I. 164-5]

These are telling, and moving, interjections. If we, through the
Bastard, take something of a comic focus on the events, through
Arthur we are brought back sharply to contemplate the inherent
pathos of them.

The statement and demonstration of the kind of right and
might asserted by John and the King of France moves, up to
Act Three, in a straight line of dramatic communication. Only
a battle could stop its relentless and unsubtle movement. It is
prevented from being boring by the presence of the Bastard and
Arthur. In Act Three, however, the straight line begins to bend
as another version of right and might is introduced in the person
of Pandulph, the papal legate. His appearance not only announces
another variation on the theme but coincides with a change in
John's character. Till now he has been little more than an example
of a monarch who, cognisant of his station, shouts his claims into
the air. From the introduction of Pandulph other qualities are
revealed.

Pandulph stands for the right of the church through the Pope as head of the Holy Roman Empire. What happens in the scene is a direct argument between one authority which has come to emphasise its power and another which does not accept that authority. In terms of true history Shakespeare has ignored the actual facts of John's relationship with the papacy. John did, indeed, submit to Innocent the Third; he was compelled to surrender his crown to Pandulph, to have it returned as a vassal, receiving it from his lord and master. The scene with Pandulph indeed expresses more directly than any other in the histories the fundamental conflict between Rome and the English reformation. In this scene the play has swerved away from its depiction of medieval power politics to an unequivocal statement of the Tudor position and the opponents of that position. In so doing Shakespeare has placed John, if only for a time, in an entirely different light. For the Elizabethan audience John, in this scene, would be naturally regarded as embodying the new-found patriotism of England itself. For the more discerning members of the audience, his reply to Pandulph would represent an affirmation of the Tudor Reformation concept of the Divine Right of Kings. The speech:

> Tell him this tale, and from the mouth of *England*
> Adde, thus much more, that no *Italian* Priest
> Shall tythe or toil in our dominions;
> But as we, under God, are supreame head,
> So under him that great supremacy
> Where we doe reigne, we will alone uphold
> Without th'assistance of a mortall hand.
>
> [III. I. 152-8]

—is clear in its declaration of the idea of Divine right.[8] John is being presented in Tudor terms, and he benefits from the translation. He is shown to be within his rights and, for a brief time, he and Tudor patriotism and belief become one.

An appreciation of political implications, however, neglects the several examples of dramatic skill which are displayed. Pandulph is a powerfully drawn character—arrogant, meticulously certain of his own argument, assured in his own status and in what he represents. Quite apart from his fluent command of the subtleties of polemical argument, he has a wry sense of timing. His words to Constance are a good example of the man. She asks him for leave to curse and says that "without my wrong/There is no tongue hath power to curse him right". He replies with a cool enunciation of the full majesty of the Church—"There's law and warrant, lady, for my curse". The whole scene is notable for dramatic irony. For example, Pandulph's arrival has come at a time when apparent amity has been found—breaches seem to have been closed, wounds licked. A marriage has been arranged. Constance's fierce agony of spirit alone infects the atmosphere. When she hears of Blanche's political betrothal, she cries out—

> Hast thou not spoke like thunder on my side,
> Been sworne my Souldier, bidding me depend
> Upon thy starres, thy fortune and thy strength,
> An dost thou now fall over to my foes?
>
> [III. I. 124-7]

Pandulph's intervention into this atmosphere reinforces what Constance's outburst has revealed—the weak expediency of these people. At a point in the play when we are becoming bored with this parade of ineffectualness Shakespeare introduces this character who has immense dramatic power, and the play is restored to some kind of order.

The theme of right has yet another form and colour in which pathos plays some part. It is embodied in Constance. When one contemplates Queen Margaret, Constance and, in this focus, brings to mind Volumnia and Lady Macbeth, it is not easy to dismiss the idea that Shakespeare had two quite distinct conceptions of womanhood. The one is best represented by Rosalind and Viola; they are the ideal and are the more precious in being rare. The other, represented by the four regal women, lies at the extreme from them. They are the female in a state of assertiveness, displaying more of the animal which, when cornered or denied of what it believes to be its right, fights with the tooth and claw of anger, grief, and cruelty. Such women are not loved for their feminity, but admired, feared, and respected for their strength of will. They dispose, to the full, a full range of devices to achieve their ends—seduction, persuasion, threat, subversion, self-indulgent emotionalism. Constance is of this breed. She has authority:

> Stay for an answer to your Embassie,
> Lest unadvis'd you staine your swords with bloud
>> [II. 1 44-5]

She is a mistress of invective:

> Doe, childe, goe to it grandame childe,
> Give grandame kingdome, and it grandame will
> Give it a plum, a cherry, and a figge,
> There's a good grandame.
>> [II. 1. 160-3]

She can make grief speak on her behalf:

> I will instruct my sorrowes to bee proud,
> For greefe is proud an't make his owner stoope.
>> [III. 1. 68-9]

She falls, vulnerable before Lewis, presents a figure of female distress and shakes his conscience with a well-timed use of the word "honour":

> His Honor, O, thine Honor, *Lewis*, thine Honor!
>> [III. 1. 316]

She has not got Richard iiird's coldly calculated ability to emulate the chameleon, but her part, in this play is, like his, based upon histrionic motivations. Nevertheless, if only in a general sense, one aspect of the theme of right is projected through her—a primitive, totally acquisitive, fierce version of the theme.

In the midst of these variations upon the basic theme stands the Bastard. He preserves our interest and patience in the whole affair. He would, one suspects, be better remembered if he existed in a better play. When he is examined in isolation he looks to be a character created with much more depth than the others. He is, like the rest, an ambitious man; to this extent he fits in with the dominating theme of the assertion of right. He gets what he wants—recognition. He delights in status, in being recognised, courted for favours. He is, in one analysis, a conceited young man, delighting in what his audacity has gained. Yet this is far from his only motivation. He will, he says, "deliver/sweet, sweet, sweet poison for the age's tooth". The sweetness of it is the delight he experiences at watching his poison work, and never so sweetly as in the way he makes the kings and warriors look foolish before the walls of Angiers. He manipulates them in a sort of war-game for his own delight:

> O prudent disciple! From North to South
> Austria and France shoot in each others mouthe:
> Ile stirre them to it . . .   [II. I. 413-15]

There is, then a dangerous mischief-making element in his character, but there is more, too. He despises those whom he can cheat and fool and sees all their actions with cynical and satirical eyes—

> Mad world, mad kings, mad composition:
> *John*, to stop *Arthurs* Title in the whole,
> Hath willingly departed with a part,
> And France, whose armour Conscience buckled on,
> Whom zeale and charitie brought to the field,
> As Gods owne souldier, rounded in the ear,
> With that same purpose-changer, that sly divel,
> That Broker, that still breakes the pate of faith.
>   [III. I. 561-68]

He has the audacious frankness of the completely amoral man. He is prepared to capitalise, for his own good, upon the way of the world as he sees it.

It is impossible, throughout most of the play, not to see in the Bastard something of that quality of cynical observation that is found in Thersites. On a simply theatrical level, both characters occupy a similar position, by reason of their soliloquies. From time to time they very conspicuously stand apart and comment, or rail, alone. The general tone of their soliloquies is similar.

Although Thersites expresses himself more venomously, both he and the Bastard are cynics, satirists, and despisers:

> And why rayle on this Commoditie?
> But for because he hath not wooed me yet:
> Not that I have the power to clutch my hand,
> When his fair Angels would salute my palme
> But for my hand, as unattempted yet,
> Like a poore beggar raileth on the rich.
> Well, whiles I am a beggar, I will raile,
> And say there is no sin but to be rich.
>
> [II. I. 587-94]

The Bastard makes himself quite plain to us. Thersites is less controlled in his cynicism, but the tone is very similar:

> How now *Thersites*? what, lost in the Labyrinth
> of thy furie? Shall the Elephant *Ajax* carry it
> thus? He beates me, and I raile at him. O worthy
> satisfaction, would it were otherwise:
> that I could beate him, whil'st he rail'd at me.
>
> [II. III. 1-5.]

They are both in pursuit of self-satisfaction; they both despise their victims; they both have a kind of honesty. Perhaps, more important, they both act as agents-provocateurs to the meaning and action of their respective contexts. The essential difference between them is that Thersite's whole function is to rail but that the Bastard is more involved in the actions upon which he looks with such a quizzical gaze. Thersites wants the world to end, so to speak, on his own terms, the Bastard wants it to continue—on his own terms.

Shakespeare, at certain points in his life, when he was dealing with themes involving disorder, human deceit, vanity, and cupidity, seems to have reacted, with different degrees of force, against his own depiction of the world, and expressed his reaction through the medium of certain characters. It is sometimes expressed loathsomely, as in Thersites, with cynical witty candour, as in the Bastard, with piquant roguery in Autolycus, and with profound fooling in *King Lear*. Such characters are no better than the world they prey or rail upon but, in their different ways, each has a more candid and realistic view of that world. It is as if Shakespeare, when confronted with some of the worlds of disorder he has created, cannot prevent himself from embodying some part of his own, intermittent, feeling that the life of man and his ways can only be regarded with a sardonic eye—that man deserves no more. Perhaps such characters embody a strain of pessimism in this basically optimistic dramatist.

The Bastard, however, offers more ground for speculation. There occurs a seemingly complete reversal of his character in the last part of the play. It requires much suspension of incredulity to equate his speeches of invective and railery with this last speech about England. If, in the first three acts he has affiliations in our minds with Thersites, by Act Five the affirming patriotic glow of Talbot and Henry v begins to shine in his words. How is this to be accounted for?

Those who find Shakespeare's patriots embarrassing, priggish, and calculating, might claim that, with the coming death of John, the Bastard himself sees the final crown of status before his eyes—the assumption of the leadership of a stricken country. There is one speech which could support an assumption that the Bastard's character is all of a piece—that the early cynic has bided his time and now, like those he has condemned, he is prepared to play the rhetorical patriotic game for his own ends:

> By all the bloud that ever fury breath'd,
> The youth saies well. Now heare our *English* King,
> For thus his Royaltie doth speake in me. . . .
>
> [v. ii. 127-9]

—a close-weaving of himself with kingship.

It is still difficult, however, to put together the man who speaks such words to Lewis, to Pandulph, and makes fools of warriors, with the man who makes a speech which, from our schooldays, we remember as one of the set-piece patriotic cries:

> . . . Naught shall make us rue,
> If England to it selfe, do rest but true!
>
> [v. vii. 116-17]

If the presence of the Bastard in the play seems equivocal, dramatically, that of King John seems unattractive, to say the least. He is the least dramatically magnetic of all Shakespeare's kings. Henry vith has a piteous and compelling dignity in his weakness; Richard iimd is curiously and potently beautiful in his vacillation; Henry ivth is of continuing interest in his conscience and grief; Henry vth is, at the least, spectacular in his self-conscious majesty; and, of all the weak or evil men, Richard iiird is compulsively powerful in his presence. King John, however, almost sidles his way through this play. Shakespeare's attempt, at one point, to use him as an emblem of Tudor patriotism and challenging power is quite unconvincing—it is rather like a cripple being unaccountably entered for the Olympic Games. It is probably because John is so dramatically effete as a character that the whole play has suffered critical disapprobation and theatrical neglect. There is, simply, no convincing kingliness in him; he lacks that one quality which all the rest of Shakespeare's monarchs, whatever their vices or virtues, have in abundance. He has a meanness of spirit and, one suspects, that if the Bastard were not beholden to him, he would be the chief target of that forthright man's invective and scorn. John is politically reckless:

> . . . see thou shake the bags
> Of hoording Abbots, imprison's angells
> Set at libertie: the fat ribs of peace
> Must by the hungry now be fed upon:
> Use our Commission in his utmost force.
>
> [III. II. 7-10]

He is unctuously cruel:

> Good *Hubert, Hubert, Hubert* throw thine eye
> On yon young boy; Ile tell thee what, my friend,
> He is a very serpent in my way,
> And wheresoere this foot of mine doth tread,
> He lies before me: dost thou understand me?
> Thou art his keeper
>
> [III. III. 59-64]

He is sanctimoniously hypocritical:

> We cannot hold mortalities strong hand.
> Good lords, although my will to give, is living,
> The suite which you demand is gone, and dead,
> He tells us *Arthur* is deceas'd tonight.
>
> [IV. II. 82-85]

He is dangerously fickle:

> Had'st thou but shooke thy head, or made a pause
> When I spake darkely, what I purposed:
> Or turn'd an eye of doubt upon my face;
> Or bid me tell my tale in expresse words:
> Deep shame had struck me dumbe, made me break off.
>
> [IV. II. 231-5]

His very death, which Shakespeare attempts to dignify by putting in his mouth words of high lyrical pathos, succeeds only in seeming a kind of petulant self-indulgence.

It is as if King John is the only monarch of English history whom Shakespeare found not only uninteresting but incapable of striking fire from his imagination. There is a sense in which one can say that Shakespeare seems to have "liked" even his most villainous king—Richard IIIrd—probably because of the attraction of his astonishing audacity, but John left him cold. John is a moral coward, unfaithful even to villainy, and everything about him goes off half-cock—it seems characteristic of Shakespeare to show a lack of warmth towards a character who lacks a positive direction in his personality; even Hamlet has the courage of his own doubts and waverings.

Because John is conceived in a cool mind the play lacks a centre; in vain Shakespeare has belatedly tried to fill the gap by raising the thematic status of the Bastard in the last act. The attempt fails because, interesting as he is, the Bastard's character is dramatically fractured—no dramatist can create a national emblem out of a convinced and convincing cynic.

It is remarkable that this play, which displays a relatively jaundiced and tired view of historical events and personages, should have been written so closely in time to the immensely virile *Henry IV*. The answer to the difference in attitude and, indeed, in artistic control, may lie in the unsolved relationship between this play and *The Troublesome Rayne*. Whatever that relationship might be, it is tempting to conclude that Shakespeare was commissioned to write a historical pot-boiler very quickly. The play has many excellent theatrical moments—it is far more viable in the theatre than is commonly supposed—but it has an uncharacteristic untidiness and fragmentation of dramatic motivation and theme. This suggests not only haste but a preoccupation with other matters. We may guess that Shakespeare was tending the growing seeds of Hal and Falstaff and impatiently dealt with this weedy plot of ground in the acres of English history.

3. *Henry IV*

Parts One and Two

The two parts of *Henry IV*[7] represent one of Shakespeare's highest achievements. When either read or seen on stage these plays have a richness of plot and theme, a grand variety of language, an exciting versatility of characterisation, which, at no point, lose a hold on our imaginations. Taken together they are, quite simply, the most consistently exciting of Shakespeare's plays. They are also much more. They represent the first absolute confirmation in the canon that the mechanical critical divisions of Shakespeare's mind and art into the divisions of comedy, tragedy, and history are superficial, misleading and irrelevant, except as convenient devices for exegesis.

In these two plays the comic, tragic, and historical visions are combined to create a many-dimensioned view of the human scene. We are not, in the presence of these plays, inclined, first to admire the sweep of historical narrative, then to gloom over the tragic figure of the conscience-stricken Henry ivth, and then to obtain relief from the gigantic comic presence of Falstaff. We may do these things in turn, but the reality of the plays lies in their interaction on each other—none of them is an insulated or isolated dramatic element.

It is partly because of the unity of his vision that Shakespeare
may be said to have provided sufficient evidence to support modern
critical claims that he conceived all of his history plays as a vast
epic of English history. Dover Wilson summarises this opinion
with certain conviction:

> When Shakespeare set forth along the road which begins
> with *Richard II*, he had the whole journey in view; had,
> indeed, already traversed the second half of it; and
> envisaged the road immediately before him, which stretched
> from the usurpation of Bolingbroke, through the troubles
> of his reign, to the final triumph of his son over the French,
> as a great upward sweep in the history of England and the
> chapter of that history which the men of his age found
> more interesting than any other. [8]

It is claimed by adherents to this view that the history plays
written before *Henry IV* seem to find their logical fulfilment
in these two parts. The fact that, historically, *Henry VI* (though
written before) follows them does not negative a belief in the
idea of an English epic. The emphasis is on the development of
certain themes, certain types of character, and on a gradually
widening and deepening conception of patriotism and of that
which constitutes a nation. Though Shakespeare, in his order of
writing, virtually reversed historical series, the *Henry IV* plays
seem to emphasise that what he was most concerned about was
not so much a connected historical account as a demonstration
of the lessons of history—the undertow beneath chronology.
Henry IV in its length and depth has, of itself, something of the
quality of epic; yet its picking-up and developing of themes and
issues, make it, in the last analysis, an epic within an epic.

It has certain, and very obvious, connexions with the earlier
histories in terms of its basic themes, yet it goes far beyond them
in the dramatic scope with which the themes are treated. Like
Henry VI, it is, to a degree, a chronicle play, designed to show
great actions performed by great men, yet it is far from confined
to the great. It takes a many-dimensioned view of human society,

and in a very unique sense. In *Henry VI* and *Richard III* areas of society below those of royalty and nobility (Jack Cade's rebellion, the citizenry of London duped by Richard of Gloucester) are depicted often with sharp observation. Yet there is a strong separation between the different areas of society. The respective inhabitants of high and low merely "visit", so to speak, those areas which are not their own. There is little co-mingling; royalty descends, looks and commands; what lives below is summoned, listens and is dismissed. In both parts of *Henry IV*, however, the kingdom is not depicted as a set of separated social areas. Each area knows its place, certainly—there is no fundamental breaking of the eternal law of class and position: but there is a far greater intercourse between one class and another. The opening of doors between high and low distinguishes this play from its predecessors and gives it a greater sense of human richness and reality. Furthermore, there is no longer the overpowering sense that what is called the commonwealth consists almost exclusively of royalty and nobility. The England of these two plays is a rich amalgam of all its citizens, both high and low.

It is connected with the earlier plays, too, in that it continues the basic themes which they have introduced and progressively developed. Divine right, rebellion, the trials of kingship, the complex of usurpation, the curse upon England, are still mute dramatis personae, but with a difference. The individual human experiences of both high and low—experiences which have to be endured inside the context of the historical themes—are given a far greater prominence.

The richness of imagination and detail which invigorates the characterisation is present also in Shakespeare's handling of the "-isms" and issues of history. In the early plays martial courage, honour, chivalry, even treachery itself, seem part of a mere ceremonial of human behaviour. In this play they become more vitally real by being subjected to an acid test which corrodes their monumental conventionality—the test of practicability at the hands of the time-serving Falstaff. No concept, no convention, no tired image or ritual, is allowed to remain in a state where its abstract presence overrides its practical validity.

An enumeration of the several elements which enrich these plays should not be allowed to obscure the amazing width of canvas upon which Shakespeare worked. Even here there is a unique quality in his handling of actual events and incidents. The two plays have a broad historical sweep but they are, uniquely, what might be described as geographical plays. England is no mere stage upon which ignorant armies clash by night and day; neither is she the suffering abstract heroine (*Res Publica*). Event has its horizontal movement traced as on a map, but the events are made more real by the fact that the map shows, in bold relief, the height and depth of the natural and human. *Henry VI* could be played upon a bare stage, and so could *Henry IV* but, in a very important sense, it demands precise indications of location. There is a greater sense of "place" about this king's court than any other's; the Boar's Head Tavern is no mere piece of visual generalisation, but is specifically a place. Even the clearer wider air of the Cotswold country demands more than a distant cyclorama and a front apron—there is cot and orchard here. Paradoxically, perhaps, the play would suffer more by being produced according to a slavish adherence to a scholarly notion of an Elizabethan stage, than by a judicious use of the resources of the modern set-designer. It does not inhibit the desires of the designer by the kind of verbal/visual indications of the chorus in *Henry V*. On the contrary its rich variety of human beings, so much part of the woof and warp of their surroundings, invites a visual evocation of that from which they have sprung. It is the fullest and most natural film-script ever written.

The plot-line is simple; it is the total length, and the variety of characterisation which deceive the audience into a belief that it has witnessed a myriad-winding plot. A king (enthroned through usurpation) is threatened with rebellion. This is met and eventually overcome. The king dies and his son assumes the crown. Insofar as Hal's adventures in the world of Falstaff can be described as a sub-plot, this consists of his meeting with Falstaff, his protection of him and his rejection of him. The play's human richness misleads the mind into believing that Hal's engagement with Falstaff is long as well as close. In fact, the intimacy of their

relationship is over and done with by the end of the Boar's Head
scene in the middle of Part One. Hal sees Falstaff only intermittently afterwards and their relationship has no more (for Hal)
than nostalgic remembrance and (for Falstaff) misplaced hope.

There are two great thematic catalysts which, by their actions,
deepen the meaning of the sparse plot-line. The first is the fact
that Henry IVth is a usurper. The true history of this king is less
that of his overcoming rebellion than of the agony of his ever-
present guilt about what he has done to get the crown. Henry
moves between an inertia brought about by conscience and a tired
activity goaded by threats to the security of what he has won.
He is a study in the pathetic irony that power ill-got corrodes the
strength and will of the begetter. Bolingbroke seized the crown
reluctantly, the dazzle of gold overpowered a certain stolid
virtuousness in the man. As Henry IVth he learns the consequences
of his actions in the form of a personal cross he has to bear;
he also knows them in an external historical sense, and he believes
that his errant son is the punishment visited on him.

> I know not whether God will have it so
> For some displeasing service I have done,
> That in his secret doome out of my blood,
> Heele breed revengement and a scourge for me.
> $$[(1) \text{ III. I. } 4\text{-}7]$$

He lives trapped, first by his guilt and second, by the suffocating
ceremony of kingship. Henry VI, a rightful king, grieves
abstractedly about the cares of the throne; Richard II creates a
poetic elegy about it; Henry IVth feels the cares in a physical sense:

> How many thousand of my poorest subjects,
> Are at this howre asleep? O sleep! o gentle sleep!
> Natures soft nurse, how have I frighted thee,
> That thou no more wilt weight my eye-liddes downe.
> $$[(3) \text{ III. I. } 4\text{-}7]$$

Henry's response to his position as usurping king gives a poignant
dimension to the events which conspire to remove him from the
throne. He himself was in Northumberland's rebellious position

after Berkeley in *Richard II*, and Northumberland himself knows the personal dimensions behind the clobbering generalities of rebellion:

> . . . let Order die,
> And let this world no longer be a stage,
> To feed contention in a lingring act:
> But let one spirite of the first borne Cain
> Reigne in all bosomes, that ech heart being set
> On bloudy courses, the rude sceane may end,
> And darknesse be the burier of the dead.
>
> [(2) I. I. 154-9]

The second catalyst is closely related with the first. Simply stated it has its existence in the irony that the heir to the usurper is considered, with apparent justification, to be feckless by his father. Because of the deeply personal reaction that Henry has to his own guilt, his response to his son's apparent insufficiency becomes deeply personal. He is not merely a tired king but a father grieving over his son's disaffection. The role of Hal as dramatic agent in the play is a very clear example of the strong emergence of a typical Shakespearean theme—that in which illusion is opposed to reality. The audience comes into possession of a knowledge about Hal which his father lacks. This, in itself, induces a classical theatrical irony, but its effect is increased by the manner in which Shakespeare enlarges the king/prince into a father/son relationship.

Thus far it is possible to see how, in general terms, the historical focus (the epic quality) and the tragic focus merge into each other. The "tragedy" of the play is in the keenly-felt guilt of Henry, representing royalty, and of Northumberland, representing rebellion, and it is present in the dramatic implications of the father/son relationship. These elements are bound together by something which casts a dark and elegiac shadow in its path. Both parts of the play demonstrate the outmoded nature both of Henry's kind of kingship and Bolingbroke's kind of rebellion. Both royalty and rebels are consanguineous in the sense that they have their being in old familiars of convention—honour, chivalry, right, even treachery (Prince John's) have about them an old inertia. In no other play is there such an impression of old and medieval concepts dying before the assaults of new concepts and ideas. The king, Hotspur, Prince John, Northumberland, are members of an older age—they exist upon thought and behaviour which Hal is to change. Falstaff cynically demonstrates how untrue to the new age these patterns are, and Hal, having learnt much from him, sets about to make kingship into a new and positive reality.

Hal is purposeful. He determines to show one face, then to replace it by the real one so that his "reformation" will seem the more spectacular. This determination is a mixture of young arrogance, vanity, and serious creative intent. It is part of his charm that it is so. There is much of the actor in him, revelling in the effects that he will have when he has taken off his make-up:

> My reformation, glittring ore my fault,
> Shal shew more goodly, and attract more eyes,
> Than that which hath no foile to set it off.
>   [(1) I. II. 206-8]

He exults in disguise; for him the best part of Gadshill is that Falstaff should not have recognised him, and when he returns to the "old frank" after Shrewsbury with Poins, his boyish delight in dressing up once again shows itself.

Yet he is actor only in part of his personality. The other part has the conscious purpose of "educating" himself into kingship. He wishes to be total king and to do this he has to make two rejections. Both of them, in different degrees, are poignant to him—his own father, as king, and Falstaff, his "adopted" father. [9]

The "rejection" of his father represents, by far, the more poignant element in these two separate relationships. It is forced upon Hal not by personal animosity but by the demands of his determination to disguise his purposes from the world. In no other play of Shakespeare's is there such a rich portrayal of a father/son relationship. It involves love, suspicion, misunderstanding, and deception and, as it is unfolded, it strikes below the

surface of the play's main theme—the secret ambitions of Prince
Hal. His conception of the meaning of kingship and the ceremony
which surrounds it is changed by his experiences and is emphati-
cally coloured by his relationships with Henry IVth. When Hal
addresses the crown at his father's bedside he looks at it with the
eyes of a realist, for he has already learned of the duplicities of
gold from Falstaff ("Never call a true piece of gold a counterfeit").
He speculates not upon its symbolic glory but upon the care it
brings to its wearer. All Shakespeare's kings have done this, but
none have made such a close personal identification between the
abstract idea of care and personal knowledge of it. "Care" and
"father" become identified for Hal:

> . . . the care on thee depending,
> Hath fed upon the body of my father.
>   [(2) IV. V. 159-60]

In this scene Hal's form of address alternates between "thee",
"majesty", and "father". For him, the crown is a repository of
majesty, awe and power, but the pain it creates is the element
which forces Hal to personalise its implications:

> . . . . I put it on my head,
> To trie with it as with an enemy,
> That had before my face murdered my father.
>   [(2) IV. V. 166-8]

The king's responses to his son maintain the level of the personal:

> O my son,
> God put it in thy mind to take it hence,
> That thou mightst the more win thy fathers love.
>   [(2) IV. V. 178-80]

Hal's rejection of his father involves a paradox which is
paralleled by the contradiction he sees in the crown itself. The
crown, to Hal, is two things: it is "the best of gold" and is "Fine,
most honour'd, most renown'd", but it is also the "worst of
gold" in that it destroys he who wears it. His father as king
corresponds to the first notion, but, as father, he is, in truth a

thing of pain, grief, and conscience. Hal responds to both, but he is torn in two, because his love for his father is equal to his determination to reject the kind of kingship which his father represents. As the action of the two plays progresses Hal does much to allay Henry's doubts about his fitness to succeed him, yet a shadow remains between the two men which prevents the personal bond from ever being completely and unbreakably connected.

The rejection of Falstaff is less poignant, though the specific act which confirms it is regarded by some critics and many theatregoers as being so. To understand the nature of and need for this rejection, it is necessary to understand Falstaff himself. He has been made into a giant by the encrustation of the sentiment of successive generations of critics and theatregoers. He has become an English monument like the Albert Memorial, whose associativeness is more countenanced than its actuality. There are indeed two Falstaffs—the character in Shakespeare's play and an image in the national imagination.

The English are characteristically drawn to show affection for men whose outward life is extrovert, hard-headed, and bonhommous, and which seems to be anchored to a shrewd, nononsense practicality of thought and feeling. John Bull seems to sum up, for the English, the values of uncomplicated opulence and simple wisdom—the results of a steady application of good sense. He is a sort of ideal businessman arriving, through astuteness, at a position where he can hob-nob with all-comers without losing a down-to-earth grasp of the facts of existence—to do better than the other man. If you substitute Falstaff for John Bull, all you need to add is an amazing way with words. Such a man has irresistible attractions for a race that prides itself in calling a spade a spade. He has a cunning penchant for self-preservation, a habit of always turning up on the leeward side of the law, an ability to collect satellite minions about him, immense in appetite and with an enviable verbal dexterity. He epitomises the ideal material man, exciting sympathy because his personality seems a pattern for all material men, and reverence because it is displayed with such largesse. He is an embodiment of that curious optimism by which material men live—wit, audacity, cheek, and expediency will see them through, they believe, anything. They do not have to be like Micawber and wait for things to turn up. While they remain cheerful and confident they make things turn up.

Because of this kind of optimism such men are vulnerable and liable to self-pity. They try to obliterate age, mutability and death by a constant use of all their powers, but intimations of these enemies make them immediately pathetic:

> Peace good Doll, do not speake like a deathes
> head, do not bid me remember mine end.
>   [(2) II. IV. 224-5]

The rejection of Falstaff by Hal has become symbolic of the kind of treachery which material men feel is likely to be inflicted by an ingrate world. Hal's reaction is called inexcusable, but for reasons often unconnected with the play itself. The logic of history means nothing to the Falstaff-idolators. They see his dismissal as a cowardly removal of what is meant by the phrase "a great guy". For them it is as if the boss has sacked the life and soul of the party just for spite; it does not matter that he is capable of wrecking the party as well as the firm. Falstaff has become the embodiment of what is called the English comic spirit because, to the English, he represents, if in an exaggerated way, the best of the English character.

J. B. Priestley's masterly essay in praise of Falstaff typifies the English attitude to this archetypal god. Hal, to Priestley, is no gentleman; his heart and mind are smaller than Falstaff's. The fat knight loves Hal but gets nothing in return. The prince goes on to Agincourt, becomes "a popular hero", a "figure for patriots in a noisy mood". Falstaff, however, goes to his own Olympus:

> Whenever the choice spirits of this world have put the
> day's work out of their minds and have seated themselves
> at the table of good fellowship and humour, there has
> been an honoured place at the board for Sir John Falstaff,

in whose gigantic shadow we can laugh at this life and laugh at ourselves, and so, divinely careless, sit like gods for an hour.[10]

This is the Falstaff that history has created, but the Falstaff who exists as a character in the play of *Henry IV* requires a less emotional approach. The most significant thing about him is that he has many acquaintances but no real friends. His minions, Bardolph, Nym, Pistol, Quickly, and Tearsheet are his victims rather than anything else. They are attracted to him like moths to a flame. They continue to circle about him more in the hope of advancement than in the expectation that the flame will do more than warm them. Pistol's presumably quick gallop to Shallow's place in Gloucestershire with the news of Hal's accession, is the action of a man who does not want to lose the main chance. Mistress Quickly's access of tears upon the departure of Falstaff to the wars is the action of a sentimental woman. Falstaff's presence in her tavern has, at least, given it a rowdy status. His departure is the end of a shoddy glory and, in any case, she is disposed, being what she is, to weep upon departure. Justice Shallow swells like a greedy sparrow in Falstaff's presence, not through affection but, first, because of that pride in association (*Sir* John Falstaff, hob-nobber with royalty, and London man to boot) and second, like the rest, in hope of advancement. Falstaff dislikes Prince John and is disliked by him. The Lord Chief Justice knows him for what he is—king of a world of commodity. The relationships of such a man depend more on head and pocket than on blood and heart.

It is the much critically maligned Hal who, alone, shows most warmth and affection to Falstaff. Priestley says that Falstaff loves Hal and that his heart is "fractured and corroborate" because of the rejection of that love. Wherein, however, does Falstaff's love lie? At no point in the play is there any proof or firm suggestion that Falstaff's relationship with Hal is, on his side, based on more than pride and avaricious expectation. When we first see them together Falstaff is in great good humour and harps about what changes, to his advantage, will occur when Hal becomes king:

Marry then, sweet wag, when thou art king let not us that
are squiers of the nights bodie be called theeves of the daies
beauty.

[(1) I. II. 22-4]

The phrase (or its equivalent) "When thou art king" rings through
the early scenes of part one like hard cash. He eagerly accepts
the playing of Hal's father in the joking game, but in order to
ingratiate himself:

There is vertue in that *Falstaffe*, him keepe with, the rest
banish.

[(1) I. I. 414-15]

If it seems critically humourless thus to judge a ripe speech in a
scene which has much comic atmosphere and intention, it is well
to recall that Falstaff himself is not merely playing a game.
When Falstaff says at the end of Act Two, scene four:

Banish not him thy Harries companie, banish plumpe Jacke,
and banish all the world.

[(1) I. I. 461-4]

Hal replies: "I do, I will." Despite the fact that the sheriff's men
are at the door, and everyone else is preparing to leave, Falstaff
will not let go. He cries: "I have much to say on behalf of that
Falstaff." Even when the hostess announces that the sheriff is
come to search the place, Falstaff does not hear her. He is too
concerned to get a satisfactory answer from Hal:

Doest thou heare Hal? never call a true piece of golde a
counterfet.

[(1) I. I. 474-5]

Throughout the play, self-aggrandisement, commodity, dominate his relationship with Hal, as it does with his minions. He is
at his height of apparent triumph when visiting Shallow. Prefer-
ment is just around the corner, but he still has his eyes upon
any material chance that presents itself. He has a clear idea of
what he can do with Master Shallow:

> I have him already tempering betweene my finger and my
> thumb, and shortly will I seale with him.
>
> [(2) IV. III. 127-8]

In contrast to Falstaff's sense of human relationship is Hal's
hard but honest procedure. On the strictly personal level he
displays a far greater unselfishness than does his giant acquaintance.
He sees that the stolen money from Gadshill is returned; he
protects Falstaff from the authorities; he is tolerant to Falstaff's
assumption of the responsibility for Hotspur's death; his speech
over the apparently dead Falstaff has a direct honesty in it:

> What old acquaintance could not all this flesh
> Keepe in a little life? poore Jacke farewell!
> I could have better spar'd a better man:
>
> [(1) V. IV. 102-4]

He does not pretend more than he says.

The rejection of this man has blinded many commentators
to the relative warmth of the Prince's feelings about Falstaff.
He takes Falstaff as he is, matching trickery with harmless fun,
but, in the doing, displaying a remarkable tolerance and affection.
Hazlitt says of the rejection: "The truth is, that we could never
forgive the Prince's treatment of Falstaff." Hazlitt speaks for
multitudes. Yet within the world of the play, two factors must
be noticed. The first is that Hal has not only made it clear that
rejection will come to Falstaff, but it should be clear to the audience
that it is necessary in order to fulfil a purpose which goes, whether
one likes it or not, beyond his own, or Falstaff's, mere personal
status. The second is that Falstaff as close intimate of King Henry
vth would have been disastrous. We must read the play, in this
respect, in the Elizabethan context which was sensitive about
anarchy, chaos, and disorder. William Empson makes this point:

> Falstaff's expectations were enormous . . . the terrible
> sentence "the laws of England are at my commandment,
> and woe to my Lord Chief Justice" meant something
> so practical to the audience that they may actually have
> stopped cracking nuts to hear what happened next . . .[11]

This point remains true whether one accepts Falstaff on a realistic or a symbolic level. Whether he be mere fat knight or Vice or Lord of Misrule, somewhere he has to end. An ambitious avaricious fat knight is dismissed; a Lord of Misrule must have a stop to his reign for it is nature's law that his carnival must end.

Yet, however much a cool summation of the fat knight reduces him from national mythology to not altogether likeable old codger (and there are a few who find him just that) even his detractors find this man, whom reason can minimise, growing in the mind as if by some mysterious process of self-generation. If you do not stay to praise him, at the very least you are compelled into laughter with him. The truth of the matter is that Falstaff, as he exists in the play, hardly has a character at all. It is possible, certainly, to summarise what he does; it is justifiable to say that he does such and such because he is a man of commodity. Yet this does not take us very far, and one realises that, in terms of the psychology of character, there is very little further that one can go. Falstaff only changes his moods; for the rest he is the same at the end as he is at the beginning. We do not receive even those darting little insights into the inside of character that we are given of some of the minor characters. His wit is a superb series of generalisations; his cowardice is a plain fact; his lying is an inevitable foible, his very pathos is predictable. What, indeed, makes even his detractors pause is something that comes from outside Falstaff, something over which he has no control. It is Shakespeare's own genius which fills an otherwise empty vessel whose shape we are given, but whose consistency and true nature we know nothing of.

Falstaff trundles away, fugitive, when one tries to turn him loose into the real world. His status as a kind of national image is dependent on the fact that he is an image—for some an ideal one. He represents what many audacious men would wish to be. However often one might be inclined, at a robust party, to see Falstaff in the fat extrovert across the room, fondling a gormless sweetie, the inclination begins to fade. It is not because Falstaff is "larger than life"—for all great dramatic creations are that. It is because none of Falstaff's characteristics add up to a sense of reality. Even those critics who have been disposed to see Falstaff in real terms are oddly prone to slip into their appraisals intimations of unreality. Thus Priestley refers to him as "a test of our sense of humour". Bradley writes of him as "the bliss of freedom gained in humour". The truth is that Falstaff is not so much witty as the expressor of Wit, he is not so much cowardly as the embodiment of Cowardice, he is not so much liar as the demonstrator of Falsehood. The situations in which he demonstrates all the matters which Shakespeare uses him for are, as it were, set up for him. Quick-wittedness is to be displayed and so we have:

> By the Lord, I knew ye as well as he that made ye. Why heare you, my maisters, was it for me to kill the heire apparant?
>
> [(1) II. IV. 259-61]

Expedient cowardice must hide its face and so we have:

> . . . Give you a reason on compulsion?
> If reasons were as plentifull as blackberries,
> I would give no man a reason uppon compulsion, I.
>
> [(1) II. IV. 231-3]

The slippery talent of lying must have its say, and there is Falstaff, the large puppet of his creator's limitless deviousness of invention, pat upon his cue:

> What art thou mad? art thou mad?
> Is not the truth the truth?
>
> [(1) II. IV. 222-3]

Falstaff's position in these plays is more important for thematic reasons than for anything else. He has to embody all the undoubtedly attractive, hypnotic usages upon which the material world exists. He fulfils this role so that Hal may learn that kingship and commonwealth do not exist upon abstractions, upon ceremony alone. Falstaff represents the vitality of day-to-day existence, the unruly comedy of its activities, the curious pathos of its determination to be more than temporary. This was the

world in which many Elizabethan Londoners had to live—
responding to the calls of appetite with the weapons of native
wit. Falstaff, the fat knight, became, in Shakespeare's lifetime,
a popular figure, not because he bestrode the stage as a recog-
nisable actuality, but because he summed up the audacious
principles and practice by which the deprived, the expedient,
and the eternally optimistic had to live.

The immensity of Falstaff's presence is capable of luring the
mind from the dramatic richness of his context. For the modern
audience Falstaff has become more important than the issues and
themes behind the actions in which he is involved. A modern
audience is not much concerned with the themes of honour,
duty, treachery, usurpation, and divine right but, as if to confirm
J. B. Priestley, to sit with Falstaff. John Wain puts it even stronger:
"He is the man we are always hoping to meet in the bar".[12]

Yet, if it were possible to set aside this man, we could realise
the immense imaginative energy that Shakespeare still had to
expend. There comes a point in every critical assessment of these
plays when the critic realises with amazement that the tremendous
comic inventiveness of the dramatist is far from exhausted by the
creation of Falstaff. In their different way the Cotswold scenes
are as powerfully achieved as the Boar's Head episode. The
stark demi-monde of London life is balanced by the shrewd
parochialism of the Cotswolds. It is in their realism that a proof
lies of Shakespeare's intimate knowledge of country ways. He
has brought to the surface the essential, almost paradoxical,
qualities of the countryman's way of thought and feeling. The
sense of generation, of the slow unchanging fundamentals of
life are here:

> Certaine, tis certaine, very sure, very sure, death (as the
> Psalmist saith) is certaine to all, all shall die. How a good
> yoke of bullocks at Stamford faire?
>
> [(2) III. I. 35-8]

Yet, commodity mixes with mutability. Together they induce a
sense of pathos which, if it were not mitigated, might eventually
become maudlin. The element which hardens their comically

senile sentimentality is the shrewd philosophy of the countryman.
This, in itself, has two aspects. The first is the eye-to-the-main-
chance materialism—an indestructible and sly cupidity. This lies
at the basis of Justice Shallow's dealings with Falstaff. The second
is a kind of pride in status and the presence of apparent status.
Shallow is in no less a state of jabbering conceit about his own
position as he is about the chance of hob-nobbing with the great
Sir John—he swells as he recalls that they heard the chimes of
midnight together. Shallow's comic richness comes from an
aspiration for equality with "greatness" which is at odds with his
doddering senility:

> The same Sir John the very same. . . . Jesu, Jesu, the mad
> dayes that I have spent! and to see how many of my olde
> acquaintance are dead.
>
> [(2) III. I. 27-33]

There is even more depth, however, to the superb realism of these
scenes. Behind Shallow and Silence stand their social inferiors—
servants and small tenants. They are not entirely allowed to
become the victims of Sir John's gigantic interruption of the
even tenor of their lives. The reluctant recruits to his troop
have all the deviousness of mind which characterises the so-called
simple peasant when he is confronted with a sophistication which
thinks it can triumph over them. Shakespeare never allows his
countryman to be bested. Soon after writing these plays he wrote
As You Like It, where the suave Touchstone is cut to size by the
shrewd and natural wit of William. Falstaff's ragged army are
not oafs:

> A horson cold sir, a cough, sir, Which I caught with ringing
> in the Kings affaires upon his coronation day, sir.
>
> [(2) III. I. 177-9]

Falstaff lords it over the Boar's Head but, in the final analysis,
he is not the lord of the Cotswolds. He may be fawned upon by
Shallow, but his measure has been taken by the humble uncommitted servant who comments on Sir John and his Company:

> No worse than they are back bitten, sir;
> for they have marvailes foule linnen.
>
> [(2) v. i. 32-4]

Shakespeare's sense of human truth is remarkably displayed here. He does not allow Falstaff to steam-roller these people. He preserves, on the one hand, the largeness of Falstaff's presence but, on the other, maintains the essential nature of these country people. This kind of balance is indeed the hallmark of these two histories. It is a balance between the insistent presence of theme and the demands of individual character. The thematic function of Falstaff is given credibility by his human relationships; the emblematic function of Hal and Hotspur—the one signifying a new order, the other an old—is given human dimension by their respective human foibles and activities; the dark issues which thematically separate King Henry and Prince Hal are made poignant and intimate by the human attributes of the father/son relationship; England, as a political concept, as *Res Publica*, is quickened into reality by the English people who crowd the plays. As John Wain[13] comments: "From the council chamber and the battlefield . . . into the lanes and hedgerows, the alleys and taprooms. And all this is faithfully carried out". *Henry IV* Parts One and Two, indeed, constitute the most comprehensive political and sociological study of a country ever undertaken— not with academic sobriety but with a full-blooded and superbly controlled artistry.

4. *Henry V*

Henry V is the most affirmatively optimistic of Shakespeare's history plays; it is also one of the most popular with audiences while, at the same time, regarded with suspicion by some scholars.

Its optimistic atmosphere is, to a very large extent, a logical outcome of Shakespeare's treatment of the themes introduced in the two plays of *Henry IV*. In those plays the curse under which England had lain since the usurpation of Richard II was still in operation. The accession of Hal, unstained by the direct guilt of his father, puts the curse in abeyance, and his reign is allowed to be productive and glorious. In this play we witness the obverse side of the fortunes which had attended England throughout the previous dark days. Where rebellion existed there is now amity; where guilt flourished there is now a pious assumption of strong kingship; where the commonweal lacked a sense of identity and unity, all is now one. Kingship freed, if only temporarily, from its bonds of guilt, now discovers an almost ideal status. Henry v is a model for a Christian monarch, kind but just, the repository of honour, aware of his duties and responsibilities to his people. He has both a regal colouring and that common touch which allows him easy commerce with high and low. The measure of his assured status is proved by the relationship which his contemporaries are shown to have with him. The church gives spiritual sanction to his military intentions; his nobility join with him in common purpose; the common soldiery find, in him, one who knows them and whom they are prepared to trust.

Thus the play is a kind of processional. It has the lineaments of a well-designed frieze which has come to life. The monarch, resplendent in perfection, leads a willing people towards the gates of success, pride, power, and patriotic fervour.

It is the quality of national epic which accounts for its popularity with audiences. It makes no great intellectual demands—we are asked merely to watch and applaud events which strike easily into our hearts. Dover Wilson[15] has caught well the nature of the play's appeal:

> But happening to witness a performance by Frank Benson
> and his company at Stratford in August or September 1914,
> I discovered for the first time what it was all about. The epic
> drama of Agincourt matched the temper of the moment,
> when Rupert Brooke was writing *The Soldiers* and the
> Kaiser was said to be scoffing at our 'contemptible' little
> army which had just crossed the Channel, so exactly that it
> might have been written expressly for it.

It is not without significance that towards the end of the 1939-1945 War the play was successfully filmed by Laurence Olivier. Its success was not entirely due to Olivier's brilliant solution of many of the problems attached to translation from stage to celluloid. It appeared at a penultimate time in the war when, after sacrifice and deprivation, there was an overwhelming sense in the western world that evil forces were near their end, that the world had been scourged and saved. In England there was a strong sense that she, by her strength, duty, and patriotic determination had, once again, achieved victory and glory. Exhaustion was tempered by pride. Bates and his confrères were easily identifiable with what the English take to be typical of their common soldiery —men given to complaint, argumentative, no respectors of person, but with stout hearts of oak. The victory of the ragged few at Agincourt was easily identified with that classic tradition that England always fights best against odds. In the period 1939 to 1945 there was no young dashing Henry to lead a proud nation. Instead there was an ageing politician, but this man knew, as did Henry, that leadership must have style. Churchill overcame the disadvantage of his age by enshrining in his speeches a spirit of virile patriotism, defiance, and contempt. He couched his sentiments in words that crossed the boundaries of age and class:

> This is no war of chieftains or of princes, of dynasties
> or national ambition; it is a war of peoples and of causes.
> There are vast numbers not only in this island, who will
> render faithful service in this war, but whose names will
> never be known, whose deeds will never be recorded.
> This is a war of the Unknown Warriors; but let all strive
> without failing in faith or in duty, and the dark curse of
> Hitler will be lifted from our age.[16]

A similar spirit pervades many of Henry's speeches:

> . . . And you, good yeomen,
> Whose limbs were made in England, show us here
> The mettle of your pasture; let us swear
> That you are worth your breeding—which I doubt not;
> For there is none of you so mean and base
> That hath not noble lustre in your eyes.

Both speeches are rhetorical in the grand manner. They have conscious style. They eschew particulars and give the hearers' emotions common denominators to respond to. Both are the voice both of the individuals who speak them and of the collective, usually inarticulate, spirit of a whole people.

The atmosphere of this play, the style of its protagonist, while it has endeared itself to audiences, has led some scholars to disapprove of it. Barrett Wendell's comment well represents the basis of this scholarly attitude:

> In the honestly canting moods which we of America inherit with our British blood we gravely admire *Henry V* because we feel sure that we ought to. In more normally human moods, most of us would be forced to confess that, at least as a play, *Henry V* is tiresome.[17]

The play has been called jingoistic and its hero priggish; its lack of intellectual depth has made it to be compared unfavourably with other, less popular, plays by Shakespeare. It appears, however, that judgment of this play—favourable or unfavourable—depends to a large extent on factors external to it. Individual political and social beliefs play the greatest part in determining critical response. The internationalist finds it reactionary, the contemplative man finds it superficial, the socialist finds it cynical, the pacifist finds it disgusting. In fact, *Henry V* celebrates the events and the feelings which embrace a nation in one of those moments of history when a nation feels it natural to think proudly of itself as a corporate whole—any jingoism it has is more the result of spontaneous pride than of calculated principle.

Henry has achieved his throne as a result of the events that took us to his coronation at the end of *Henry IV* Part Two. The preparation for the kind of king he is to be has been carefully made and presented to us:

> The breath no sooner left his Fathers body,
> But that his wildnesse mortify'd in him,
> Seem'd to dye too: yea, at that very moment,
> Consideration like an Angel came,

And whipt th'offending *Adam* out of him;
Leaving his body as a Paradise,
T'invelop and containe Celestiall Spirits.   [I. I. 25-31]

The motto of the play might well be the words of Ely: "We are blessed in the change".

When we see Henry at the beginning of the play, all doubts have gone—he is in unquestioned majesty. It is as if what now remains is the palpable proof of his status as great king. This proof, which the play is to unfold, will confirm Hal's melodramatically-expressed intention to surprise by reform at the beginning of *Henry IV* Part One. There is an air of relaxed and confident expectation at the play's beginning which is given some piquancy by the long speeches of the two ecclesiastics. Nowadays it is difficult to accept their long essays into legal niceties without a smile, yet it is essential that what they have to say about Henry's claims and the Sallic law should be taken seriously, as indeed the Elizabethans did. For them, the speeches would not have been taken as semi-comic pedantics, muttered and sipped by two ageing clerics. They were sensitive to matters concerning right and succession, they were less impatient to listening to the rolling logic of unquestioned authorities than are we but, more important, Henry's claim was regarded as historically justified. Unless Henry's adventure in France is to be regarded as an illegal act, the cleric's speeches must be listened to. If Henry's adventure in France is regarded as illegal then the play's patriotism and pride, its picture of a unified nation, can only be a bad and cynical joke. As Arthur Humphreys says:

> The Archbishop's prominence and Henry's earnest
> injunctions to him 'justly and religiously' to state the case
> are meant as proof that the claim is lawful and French
> resistance to it unlawful, so that by contumacy France
> provokes an 'impious war' not only against her rightful
> sovereign but against God, the source of royal authority.[18]

In short, for Shakespeare's dramatic and thematic purpose, Henry must not only be, but be seen to be, the true image of a Christian king.

Throughout the play a sense of ordered legality about actions that are taken is emphasised. The judgment on the three traitors at Southampton cannot be regarded merely as an emblematic clearing up of one dark corner in an otherwise consenting kingdom—a kind of tidying up towards unremitting perfection; it has other implications. The story of Henry v was well-known, the conspiracy of Cambridge, Scroop, and Grey was accepted as having happened in fact.

Many in the audience would know this history and, for those, this episode would have a special meaning. For those who lacked the knowledge the scene would have the general effect of reminding them of the frequent threats by traitors to their own monarch's life. It is worth remembering that Shakespeare emphasises that the judgment on them is the result of the application of a severe but fair law—which the traitors themselves had appealed to.

The sense of an utter correctness of behaviour by this royal Henry is intensified by his Christian piety. His decision to enter France is approved by law and by invoking the blessing of God. The intercession and approval of the Almighty is sought many times in the play, not least in those speeches when Henry questions himself and speculates upon the duties and responsibilities of kingship. The scene with the common soldiers before Agincourt gives us perhaps the most intimate and warm experience of this Christian king—he steps out of the image of Christian king and is revealed in the personal and solitary reality of a confrontation with his maker:

> O not to day, thinke not upon the fault
> My Father made, in compassing the Crowne
> [IV. I. 289–90]

This king's piety is not a simple dedication to the will of God nor a jingoistic assumption of God's blessing, for it has within it a powerful penitential motive—Henry is not, as some critics would have him, the cold hero who, by military prowess, restores England's fortune; his actions are a conscious aid to penitence—he leads his people to glory and, he hopes, to expiation:

> ... More will I doe:
> Though all that I can doe, is nothing worth;
> Since that my Penitence comes after all,
> Imploring pardon.
>
> [III. I. 298-301]

The play, in its concentration on the legal correctitude of royal action, and on the sanction of the Almighty, mirrors an order which, as it were, encompasses the kingdom of heaven and of earth. It is in sharp contrast to the disorder of *Henry VI*, *Richard III* and, to a lesser extent, *Henry IV*. In this play there are no references to malevolent stars, no hints that the planets wander in disorder. Such references would be superfluous, since God has now chosen to direct England's path towards order and unity. For the moment he smiles on England. The play is an integral part of the design of Shakespeare's history plays—the historical process is still being demonstrated:

> O God, Thy Arme was heere;
> And not to us, but to Thy Arme alone,
> Ascribe we all.
>
> [IV. VIII. 104-6]

It is a logical continuation of the *Henry IV* plays in another respect. Quite clearly, Henry V is an older and wiser Prince Hal. The play shows an ordered and unified commonwealth, but it also reveals the practical results of Hal's actions and motivations in *Henry IV*. The Prince's education into kingship, self-imposed, is now complete. The play is, so to speak, his graduation ceremony. This has several aspects, but its most certain emphasis is on the fact of Hal's "reformation" from wild boy to glorious king. This emerges, not only in the general celebrative atmosphere of the play, but in the references that are made to the king. His own demonstration of the completeness of his reformation is affirmed by both speeches and imagery:

> A largess universal as the sun.
> Never was monarch better feared and loved
> Than is your majesty.
> The Lord in heaven bless thee, noble Harry!

Hal's education involved the rejection of two mentors—his father and Falstaff. His succession involves a return to royal status which is of a different kind from that inhabited by his father or envisaged by Falstaff. His occupancy of the throne is based on a knowledge which he has learned from both but it necessarily involves the rejection of both. The play of *Henry V* gives ample evidence of the "knowing" which Hal has achieved. It is conveyed, for example, with telling force in the speech which contains the lines:

> ... And I know,
> 'Tis not the Balme, the Scepter, and the Ball,
> The Sword, the Mace, the Crowne Imperiall,
> The enter-tissued Robe of Gold and Pearle,
> The farced Title running 'fore the King,
> The Throne he sits on: nor the Tyde of Pompe,
> That beates upon the high shore of this Worlde:
> No, not all these, thrice-gorgeous Ceremonie;
> Not all these, layd in Bed Majesticall,
> Can sleepe so soundly as the wretched Slave;
> Who with a body fill'd, and vacant mind,
> Gets him to rest, cram'd with disstressefull bread.
>
> [IV. I. 255-66]

The "I know" in these lines is no empty remark. Its existence in the speech, if taken in conjunction with our own knowledge of the Hal of the previous plays, irradiates the whole meaning of Hal's words about kingship. Without these words and our own experience of Hal, it is a mere set-piece, typical of those uttered by Shakespeare's kings about the cares of the throne. The "I know" makes all Hal's words simply but profoundly factual.

The comprehensiveness of this new kind of kingship is proved by Henry's ability to talk naturally with his common soldiers. Words like "honour", and "duty", which exist in the previous histories as mere abstractions, have a different status in this play because they are proved by experience and action. Henry's duties as king are not merely clearly defined but shown in action. Honour emerges in the depiction of Henry's high standard of honesty, right judgment, and nobility of mind; it appears equally with high-born and low-born. Duty and responsibility are embodied in the care which Henry has for his subjects and in his ability to question his own motives for action. In this king abstractions are turned into realities, and they are given an urgency by the existence of conscience in the man which constantly reminds him of the necessity to act correctly as an atonement for the sins of his father.

Yet Henry is not a mere and perfect embodiment of the ideal king. It cannot be denied that there seems to be a calculating quality in the man. The first scene of the play is the best example of this. It is implicit that Henry is determined to go to France whatever the legal conclusions of the bishops. It is true also, as Traversi says, that "He has a willingness to shift the responsibility upon others, to use their connivance to obtain the justification which he continually, insistently requires". Traversi notes that Henry warns Canterbury that, before war is let loose, he must have a care that the decision is not lightly taken:

> For we will heare, note, and beleeve in heart,
> That what you speake, is in your Conscience washt,
> As pure as sinne with Baptisme.

> [I. II. 28-32]

For the actor there is sufficient textual justification to interpret Henry as something of a young éminence grise who bends (as in the wooing of Kate) only with difficulty towards a relaxation of will and purpose. Yet such an interpretation would still have to take into account certain elements in his character by which Shakespeare mitigates the impression of inflexibility and humanises this king.

It is worth emphasising that Henry is an older and wiser Hal, but there is the same proportion of the younger man left in him as there is of Prince Richard in *Richard III*. In order to assess the place of this in the character it is necessary to examine other reminders of the play of *Henry IV* which remain.

Falstaff is a mere nostalgia—as indeed are all the rest of the Boar's Head crew, with the exception of Pistol. When the master goes the rest very quickly become expendable, but it is important to realise how they are despatched. Bardolph is hanged, Nym disappears, Poins never appears, and Pistol, though he is more sharply characterised, is relegated from bombast to cut-purse. In this play he is, indeed, shown for what he is; without the presence of Falstaff the comedy that remains in him cannot swell, but is thin and circumscribed. The conclusion cannot be escaped (and performance always emphasises this) that the remnants of the Boar's Head are deliberately cleared away, and are seen to be cleared away, so that no suspicion of a connexion of the old order with the new Hal may be entertained. One short scene alone (and this only by implication) gives a catch to the memory of the old Frank. It is the killing of the boy (who has, in many productions, been identified with Francis the drawer) by the retreating French. Nothing else interferes with the emergence of the new king. It is on this point that one's opinion about the personality of the king hinges. The accusation of cold priggishness depends on a sentimental assumption that it is Henry V who rejects all the remnants of the old life. This is wrong. It is Shakespeare who wills them away for his own dramatic purposes. The important point is that he takes precautions against the possibility of what is left seeming unremittingly and unattractively perfect. The attractive but corruptive comedy of the Boar's Head is replaced by the affirmative comedy of Fluellen. His comedy, in itself, is, as it were, based on generalisations—the typed Welshman speaking typed language. By comparison with the comedy generated in the halcyon days of Falstaff it is, so to speak, safe, warm, and, in the long run, good natured. Yet what is important about Fluellen's presence is Henry's response to it. In his dealings with his fellow-countryman Shakespeare is careful to show Henry revealing more than mere glimpses of a playfulness of spirit, a gamesomeness. Through this we are made to recognise that something of the younger prince still lurks in the older king. It is difficult to escape the conclusion that what is allowed to emerge in the Fluellen relationship, and in the wooing of Kate, is deliberately contrived to humanise the presence of Henry in the play. If, in performance, these relationships are minimised, a charge of priggishness may stand. Their presence, and the emphasis given to them, does not only negate the charge but positively affirms the kind of king that Hal educated himself to be—total in all the appurtenances of majesty, and in human response.

Concentration on Shakespeare's working out of the pattern which has its genesis in *Henry IV* tends to bend the mind towards the English world of the play to the exclusion of the French. Shakespeare, however, shows remarkable dramatic balance in the overall design of the play. The French scenes and the French characters are among some of his best creations at this period in his working life. His main achievement is to satisfy the audience's contempt for the hated and decadent French without losing a hold on credibility. The French are individualised with remarkable and economic skill. The Dauphin is dangerous and self-indulgent, the Constable a cynical realist, the King fearful and feeble. Even the French Herald is strongly outlined. He is a model of duty and courtesy and is also a wry emblem of an old order which is to receive its death blow at Agincourt. These men, added together, create a picture in depth. The French world is not set up as a mere Aunt Sally for the glorification of England; it exists as a dramatic entity in its own right; its posture as victim has an intensely human as well as a thematically inevitable quality. Shakespeare's manipulation of the French and English worlds goes beyond simple contrast. There is nothing mechanical about the manner in which he depicts the virtues of the one and the weaknesses of the other, and the two scenes before the battle of Agincourt are a telling example of subtlety of dramatic grasp. What deepens the general contrast between the atmosphere of the two camps is the absence of French common soldiery. This places the French nobility in a position of curious isolation, whereas Henry is seen as gathering about him a small but affirmative fellowship. This heightens the dramatic effect but also emphasises the difference between a complete and an incomplete commonwealth. In the long run, what we are shown, in the juxtaposition of English and French worlds before the battle, is the difference between virile youth and crabb'd age, between a new dynamic political and military order and one that is old and outworn. Henry, having been shown as growing out of the outworn Englishness of his father's court, is thus revealed in a larger context.

Henry V was the last (save for the doubted *Henry VIII*) English history play to be written by Shakespeare. His long committal to English history ends with a flourish which is so grand that it is tempting to believe that he had decided that it was time to cease his wrestlings with a mode that had occupied him for so long. By comparison with the other histories, including the immature *Henry VI*, the play is lacking in dramatic abrasiveness, in irony, and in tragic implications. The cynic might observe that, for Shakespeare, English history, having gone through hell, ends not in heaven so much as at a mighty fête. It is fair to conclude, however, that, within the large series, its themes have a logical and natural place and that, in itself, it gives evidence of a far greater dramatic skill than its detractors allow.

3

COMEDY

1. *The Merry Wives of Windsor*

A ghost of Falstaff appears in *The Merry Wives of Windsor*. General critical opinion of the play—that it is a happy trifle—is bedevilled by the nature of this ghost.

The Falstaff of Windsor Park is not the Falstaff of Gadshill, the Boar's Head, and Shrewsbury clock. By comparison, he has bated and pined. Commentators seem reluctant to accept the play on its face value—a clever piece of light entertainment—because they seem nostalgic for a man who once reigned like an emperor and now does not. Hazlitt's view is typical:

> [It] is no doubt a very amusing play, with a great deal of humour, character, and nature in it: but we should have liked it much better, if any one else had been the hero of it, instead of Falstaff.[1]

Again, some critics seem put off by the fact that this is the only comedy in the canon whose action takes place specifically in England, and concerns itself almost exclusively with virile middle-class tradespeople. It is as if there is a reluctance to believe that Shakespeare was capable of "stepping down", both in his depiction of Falstaff and in his use of a social class which is conspicuously absent from the rest of his plays. Georg Brandes, writing of the necessity to entertain the Queen and her Court at Windsor refers, somewhat haughtily, to the amused pleasure the monarch had in catching a glimpse of a class so remote from her own, and he adds: "Thus it became more prosaic and bourgeois than any other play of Shakespeare's".[2] As if to exonerate the playwright he draws attention to the introduction of fairy dance and song at the end of the play, since he "found it impossible to content himself with thus dwelling on the common earth".

Apart from the interest which Falstaff and the use of the middle class has, and should have, for the critic, the play has other intriguing facets. One is the occasion of its first performance; another is the possibility of hidden biographical details, and a third is the depiction of the Welshman, Sir Hugh Evans.

Peter Alexander writes that "the date 23rd April, 1597 for the first performance of *The Merry Wives* is probably one of the few dates in the chronology we can be confident about".[3] Leslie Hotson has convincingly suggested that it was written for a performance to celebrate the Garter Feast of St George's day.[4] On this occasion new Knights were inducted into the Garter order and, following a banquet at Greenwich, their installation took place at Windsor Castle. He further suggests that there is a specific reference to the preparations for the installation in the Fairy Queen's words:

> Each fair instalment, coat, and sev'ral crest,
> With loyal blazon, evermore be blest!

There may have been a special reason for commissioning Shakespeare to write for the occasion, because the patron of his company—the Lord Chamberlain's—was himself received into the order in 1597. A deal of evidence points to Shakespeare's having been asked to write a special play for the occasion:

> This comedy was written at her command, and by her direction, and she was so eager to see it Acted, that she commanded it to be finished in fourteen days and was afterwards, as Tradition tells us, very pleas'd at the Representation.[5]

It is very tempting to accept the idea that Shakespeare, having been asked to recall Sir John and, casting around for a plot, allowed his mind to wander around the actual place where the celebrations were to take place. A fat knight had to be brought back from his grave to please a Queen, but there were other knights to hand—those to be installed in St George's chapel. Windsor, like the Stratford of his youth, was a place where a thrifty, hard-working middle class, was surrounded by the suave elegance of knightly families. The Queen's progress to Warwick in 1587 had attracted high and low to witness the pageantry. The local knights, he may have recalled, were agog to display themselves to their monarch. One, in particular, whose graceful estate was a short walk from Henley Street, might very well have come into his memory—Sir Thomas Lucy. In the first scene of the play Shallow enters and says that Falstaff has poached his deer, and he adds, talking of his ancestors:

> They may give the dozen white Luces in their Coate.
>
> [I. I. 13-14]

To which Evans replies:

> The dozen white lowses doe become an old Coat well.
>
> [I. I. 16-17]

The pun on "luce" and "louse" is obvious. Sir Thomas Lucy bore luces on his armorial insignia; if the story of Shakespeare's deer-poaching at Charlecote is true (and though it is unauthenticated it is feasible) then, in his mind, an association between luce and louse would be natural—if Sir Thomas's reaction was as stinging as it is likely to have been.

The other possibly biographical matter centres on Sir Hugh Evans. Much play has been made of the appointment to the mastership of the Grammar School of Thomas Jenkins in 1575, and it was widely believed that Sir Hugh Evans is based upon this man. Jenkins left the school in 1597 under something of a cloud, and the nineteenth century conjectured that his departure was the result of certain tactless qualities which Shakespeare displays, but mellows, in Sir Hugh. But all this may be an example of a wish fathering a thought. In the first place little is known of Jenkins except that he was educated at St John's, Oxford; more disappointing to those who wish to perpetuate the connexion with Sir Hugh, it is possible that Jenkins was, in fact, a Londoner. The connexion, indeed, remains a very open one.

What can be said with confidence is that the scenes in which Sir Hugh appears are very sharply observed; they have the effect of actual memories of a schoolmaster—Welsh or not. Sir Hugh is, without doubt, a pedantic pedagogue, but his Welshness derives from certain popular Elizabethan notions of what Welshmen were like. They were regarded as Bible-thumpers, shrewd, not to say devious, unless they were watched; they could be conceited in their knowledge (Fluellen gives evidence of this) and were marvellous wondrous in their use and misuse of the English language.

The dignified and extrovert religiosity of Sir Hugh, and his disingenuous worldly shrewdness is well-drawn in the first scene:

> I am of the church, and will be glad to do my benevolence, to make attonements and compremises betweene you.
> [I. I. 27-30]

> . . . seven hundred pounds of Moneyes, and Gold, and Silver, is her Grand-sire upon his deaths-bed (Got deliver to a joyfull resurrections . . .)
> [I. I. 46-49]

Like the important Divine that he believes himself to be, he assumes the status of uncommitted arbiter; like the shrewd Welshman that he is, he keeps his eye on worldly chances:

> I, and her father is make her a petter penny.
> [I. I. 53-4]

He is also given to melancholy and song—two attributes long considered to be inhabitants of the Welsh soul. Yet he never forgets his dignity:

> Pray you, let us not be laughing-stocks to other men's humours.

But the finest of Sir Hugh is seen in the education of his pupil, William. Here, Shakespeare has seized upon the conceit of learning and turned it into superb comic usage:

EVANS: . . . What is *Lapis William*?
WILL: A Stone.
EVANS: And what is a Stone *William*?
WILL: A Pebble.
EVANS: No, it is *Lapis* . . .

[IV. I. 28-31]

The interplay between Quickly and Evans in this scene is a fine example of Shakespeare's sharpness of eye for human foibles. Quickly's outraged sensibilities do, in fact, protest themselves too much; overtly she is shown as being no better than she is. Evans's ripostes bespeak the large but flimsy dignity of one who wears his status on his sleeve.

Shakespeare probably did not know the Welsh language, but his ear for the Welshman speaking English is acute and precise. The tendency to use words for their dramatic effects he has seized upon; the tendency to drop the initial "w" is unerringly shown; the absence of the letter "v", and the occasional habit of using a noun instead of a verb or an adjective—these, too, he pinpoints, so that Evans's speech is nearer actuality than caricature.

The play, then, is fascinating for matters which are contiguous to Shakespeare's own life and experience of people. Yet, in the end, it is the appearance of Falstaff which arouses the deepest interest. He is, in every way, a diminished man and character. The thematic and actual world he inhabits seems smaller; his relationship to his surroundings and to others is significant only as a cog in the mechanics of the whole play; his wit lacks the enormous variety, subtlety and point which the old Falstaff commanded. Above all there is no Prince Hal against which he can measure himself, and, in so doing, swell into his own ego. He has, as it were, dragged remnants of his former court with him into this play—Shallow, Bardolph, Pistol, Nym, and Quickly, but his relationship to them—overweening domination —is now quite put down. It is tempting to conjecture that this Falstaff is very much the one who lives in debt and vilification following the rejection by Hal. His status in the world of Henry IV depended on his own large but quite fragile expectations of plenty and position in the new kingdom. Those expectations were completely confounded and this Falstaff is the result. The sycophancy and patience shown by his followers depended on their hope that he would pull them all into glory and money behind him. The very first lines of this play starkly show what happens when the star they hitched themselves to is fallen:

> . . . If he were twenty Sir *John Falstaffs*, he shall not abuse *Robert Shallow* Esquire.
>
> [I. I. 3-4]

We hear that Falstaff has "committed disparagements", that "the council shall hear it", but his first appearance gives some hope that the ghost has something of the old substance left in him:

> SHALLOW: Knight, you have beaten my men, kill'd my deere, and broke open my Lodge.
> FALSTAFF: But not kiss'd your keeper's daughter.
>
> [I. I. 100-1]

But this is no more than a flash. He cannot control events or people as he used to. The scene at the Garter Inn is a thin image of the great days at the Boar's Head—the braggadocio language has a tired edge to it. What is significant about this scene is the decision of Falstaff to woo Ford's wife in an attempt to get her husband's money. The old Falstaff would, one is assured, have been no less ready to enter a stratagem for profit. But the old Falstaff would never have committed himself so explicitly to it; he would have hedged about his intentions, and deployed all the forces of his language, imagination and devious intelligence to make a subterfuge. This ghost, desperate for money, puts his cards upon the table, and they are picked up by, of all people, Pistol. Falstaff is become a mere character in a comic intrigue and, as if to emphasise his diminution, Pistol and Nym decide to reveal his plot.

The whole of the history of Falstaff in this play is that of how he is revenged *upon*. This we never see in *Henry IV* (even Hal's revelations about what really happened at Gadshill are turned by Falstaff to comic advantage). Until the final rejection, Falstaff reigns supreme in the world of Henry IV, precisely because he is not brought to any final challenge. He seems the bigger for this; in this play he seems the smaller because people are given the chance to "consult together against this greasy knight".

There is no more telling comment on the smaller dimensions of Falstaff than his own words to Pistol:

> I myselfe sometimes, leaving the feare of God on the left hand, and hiding mine honor in my necessity, am fain to shuffle: to hedge, and to lurch.
>
> [II. I. 21-4]

Yet his diminution has another aspect to it. Tremendous visual emphasis is put on his visual discomfiture and, unlike Gadshill, he is not given the verbal resources to redress the balance against him. He is placed in a basket, he is ducked in a river—he becomes a figure to whom things are done, and therefore becomes a mere agent in a plot-line:

> I am not able to answer the Welch Flannell . . . use me as you will.
>
> [V. V. 155-7]

He *is* used as they will and is absorbed mechanically in the play's devious plot and happy resolution. The ghost of the man who "larded the earth" is invited by Page to "eat a possett" at his house, to "laugh at my home, where I will desire thee to laugh at my wife that now laughs at thee". All are invited "to laugh this sport o'er by a country fire" by Mrs Page, and she adds "Sir John and all". It is as if Shylock accepted the stern invitation to become Christian—like Falstaff he would have gone out of his proper element.

The iron political and thematic necessities of Shakespeare's *Henry IV* require Falstaff's annihilation; the demands of the plot in *The Merry Wives* require a scapegoat. He is, in modern parlance, an all-time loser. In a sense the real death of Falstaff happens when he is asked to sit by the fire and join in laughter. This is a domestic procedure which suits well the dénouement of this play with this Falstaff, but it is mocked by memories of what the other Falstaff would have done with such laughter.

The class which defeats him is one which Shakespeare had never before exploited, on this scale, in his plays. We associate its people with Dekker and Jonson but not with him. Their reality as a contemporary class in Elizabethan society is, indeed, more shrewdly revealed by those two dramatists than by Shakespeare. He avoids any close analysis and concentrates on supplying generalities necessary for the furtherance of the plot. Their morality is straightforward, their humour limited and broad, their intelligence circumscribed, their threshold of tolerance of human foibles not large. The individuals who constitute this class do not give the actor or actress any opportunity for more than broad comic playing, and the situations that surround them are patterned on the quick to-ing and fro-ing of farce. Doors open and close quickly, arrases hide anxious men, swift and ludicrous decisions are constantly being made. All, indeed, points to very swift preparation and writing—Shakespeare had no time for niceties of characterisation or incident. The main requirement is that the play should be merry.

It is on this point of merriment that one's experience of the play turns. Taken *per se*, it is a farcical series of episodes in which a biter (Sir John) is bit. It has a mellow and pleasing theatrical conclusion. The "villain" is brought to heel and finally joins the happy dance. It is not difficult to imagine that first night audience applauding the antics, hissing the villain, and delighting in the reconciliatory ending, with its acceptable touch of the supernatural world.

At the same time one wonders whether there might not have been some, perhaps the Queen among them, who found it difficult to detach the play from their recent memories of the past. Towards the end Falstaff, shrived of his misdemeanours, is surrounded by those who have defeated him. He turns to Evans and says:

> Have I liv'd to stand at the taunt of one that makes Fritters of English? This is enough to be the decay of lust and late-walking through the Realme.
>
> [v. v. 138-40]

Falstaff, in other days, demolished anyone with his own inspired frittering of the language; he lusted for the rewards of commodity, and thrived on expectation but, more than anything, he late-walked through the realm of England and an heir-apparent walked at his side. Any member of any audience who has known *that* Falstaff cannot quite join in the delightful merriment of this play. It may seem sententious, when one is faced with a pleasing trifle like this play, to think of richer matters, yet Shakespeare's mind was of a piece, and his creation of Falstaff so strong that we cannot help but see Falstaff all of a piece. He responded to the Queen's demand for a play and diminished Falstaff for her pleasure. She would have been characteristically insensitive if her merriment had not been tinged with sadness.

2. *A Midsummer Night's Dream*

If any confirmation were needed of the versatility of Shakespeare's genius in his early days in the London theatre, *A Midsummer Night's Dream* would provide it. It not only stands in sharp thematic and stylistic contrast to the early histories, with *The Merchant of Venice*, and with *The Merry Wives of Windsor*, but it has, within itself, an amazingly disciplined variety of characterisation, language, and atmosphere. The realistic eye which informs the creation of the mechanicals is matched by the romantic gaze which produced the lyric fantasy of the world of Oberon and Titania, and the inconsequentialities of the two pairs of lovers. Yet, remarkably, the play is all of a piece—the changes of pace, style, and character-types are all held within a tender and sensitive grasp; it is a play of love which is lovingly written.

Like others of Shakespeare's plays (notably *The Merchant of Venice* and *The Tempest*) its popularity with audiences seems to depend upon a simplification of what, on closer study, seems to be relatively complicated, both structurally and thematically. With those two other plays, it has taken an honourable place in audience's affections because it has certain obvious affinities with a fairy-story. It is regarded as a fantasy-fable whose function is simply to lure the mind and affections away from the tribulations of ordinary existence into a world where all will be well and where, by magic, anything is possible. If all our dreams could be guaranteed to be like this play, then many of us would be for ever sleeping.

While such an image of the play has obvious confirmations in many of its inherent qualities it is, nevertheless, a simplified image, and the stage-history proves the tenacity of an uncomplicated audience-acceptance.

Betterton's version in 1692 re-titled it *The Fairy Queen*, with music by Purcell. Garrick vamped it into a "new English opera" in 1755, called it *The Fairies* and introduced twenty-eight songs. When Ellen Terry was eight years old she appeared as Puck, and made her first entrance from a trap-door seated on an artificial mushroom. In 1929 Harcourt Williams's production at the Old Vic introduced specially written folk-tunes and dressed its fairies in imitation sea-weed. Robert Helpmann danced his way through the character of Oberon and, as late as 1959, Peter Hall, though he attempted to modernise the lovers' comedy, somehow contrived to imitate nineteenth-century opulence with his gauze-shrouded set and bosky woodland.

The stage-history is dominated by attempts to minister to audience-expectation of lush fantasy. Moreover, through the centuries, versions have threaded golden notes of sound to complete the fantastic pattern. Mendelssohn who, over seventeen years, was captivated by the play and wrote, in that period, the various parts of his incidental music, is only one of the most celebrated of many who have embroidered the play. John Smith wrote incidental music in 1755; Louis Spohr made an opera of it in 1826; Hugo Wolf wrote songs for it in 1881 and, in 1960, Benjamin Britten was inspired to compose his celebrated operatic version.

In the face of this record, there can be small wonder that the play has held, for audiences, the status of fantasy and magic, spiced, but never drenched, with the homespun comedy of the very English mechanicals. Neither is it surprising, on the contrary, that, very recently, there have been evidences of a reaction to this traditional treatment of the play. The mode for what was termed "sharp satire" in both television and stage entertainment in the mid-1960s affected certain productions—notably Peter Hall's at the R.S.T. in 1961 and David Scase's at the Nottingham Playhouse in 1967. In both cases (though with far greater expertise in the former) the play was subjected to a contemporary kind of debasement. The fairy-world was self-mocking, the lovers were "modernised" by a studied avoidance of cadence in speaking, and by a glib assumption of contemporary gestures. In both cases, in varying degree, the play was used, in a sense, to guy itself. In the Hall production the result was a superbly entertaining travesty, in the Scase production an inefficient vulgarisation. Neither production would, in itself, merit much notice except that they are indicative first, of the general movement towards the "contemporising" of Shakespeare in the sixties and, second, of the vulnerability of this particular play to mockery and guying. It requires a most sensitive style of interpretation and acting to preserve its quite fragile thematic balance. The director who decides to "style" it from any single one of its apparently separate ingredients (The Court or The Fairy World or Bottom's world) is doomed to fracture its delicacy of structure. The problem for the director is to apprehend and to hold on to its persistent thematic tone. This has different appearances and emphases in the various revealed worlds of the play, but it informs them all and, in the end, is seen as a unifying force. It is the nature of this unifying force which must inform any claim that the play is more than mere fairy-tale stuff.

Some modern critics have sought to identify the thematic heart of the play in terms which, in the end, might seem to neglect the Elizabethan reality of the play. Jan Kott, for example, finds a hideous and dark symbolism in it. With a ferocious sincerity he has allowed a twentieth-century partisan outlook to denude the play of the one quality which commends it—its ability to please, to make content.

> *The Dream* is the most erotic of Shakespeare's plays. In no
> other tragedy or comedy of his, except *Troilus and Cressida*
> is the eroticism expressed so brutally.[6]

Yet, what, in mythological, or even psychological, terms may
be complicated is, in dramatic terms, quite simple. A dream may
induce layers of explanation from modern exegesis but, as an
entity in itself, can be, like Shakespeare's play, a plain statement
of essentials:

> Thinke but this (and all is mended)
> That you have but slumbred here,
> While these visions did appeare.
> And this weeke and idle theame,
> No more yielding but a dreame.
> [V. I. 413-17]

The theme is far from idle and weak, though its surface actions
may seem no more than a series of playful arpeggios.

The occasion considered as most likely for the play's first
performance is generally accepted as the wedding of Elizabeth
de Vere, the daughter of the Earl of Oxford, to the Earl of Derby,
in January 1595. Its creation for a particular ceremony would
seem to justify a conclusion that it was intended as no more than
light entertainment. Indeed the narrative line, and the ending,
could be taken to reflect the style and atmosphere of its first
audience. All proceeds towards the end of marriage; the world
of lovers is blessed by a fairy world whose master and mistress
have themselves rediscovered their own love for each other.
There is a strong element of ceremonial both in the action and
in the self-conscious ritual of some of the language. Some
commentators, however (including its most recent editor[7]) believe
that it was always intended for public performance, and that the
presence of Bottom and his fellows suggests that it was intended
for popular rather than private consumption.

The nub, as so often in these matters, is the date of composition.
Its place in the canon is uncertain, though it is generally regarded
as being later than the early comedies and that it pre-dates *Romeo
and Juliet*. A quarto version appeared in 1600, but the consensus
of opinion is that it was completed in 1594. No direct source
has been discovered; this might be taken to support the idea that
Shakespeare, faced with a special occasion, relied on his own

invention. The play bears little signs of haste in the writing, though there is stylistic unevenness. This, however, suggests rewriting rather than hasty composition.

Although no direct source has been discovered, Shakespeare certainly drew on his knowledge of a number of books. The complicated wooing tale was a convention of Italian comedy; the story of Theseus and Hippolyta is found in Chaucer's *The Knight's Tale*. Shakespeare may also have read a version of the life of Theseus in North's translation of Plutarch. His memory of school text-books may have recalled the story of Pyramus and Thisbe in Ovid's *Metamorphoses*. J. Dover Wilson believes that Bottom's affair with Titania owes something to the story of Cupid and Psyche in Apuleius's *The Golden Ass*. For the rest— the mechanicals and fairies—he need have looked no further than to his experience and his imagination. All the mechanicals have trade names that Shakespeare would have come across in his native Warwickshire; all the attendant fairies are, in their simple functions, closely related to the beliefs of country life. It should be emphasised, however, that, in temperament, they are not in line with the commonly accepted beliefs of the time. Fairies were mischievous beings who interfered in human activities, usually to embarrass or to set those activities in disarray. They were often vicious and spiteful, but the best known was Robin Goodfellow (Puck) who was regarded as more mischievous than evil. Shakespeare has stuck very closely to the conventional and traditional characteristics of Puck but, as if to conform to the happy tenor of his play, has made the lesser fairies positively benevolent— innocently inoffensive.

Their nature and size raises problems about the way in which they were originally staged and how, nowadays, they should be staged. There is no reason to disbelieve that, if the play were written for a private performance at a wedding ceremony, the parts were taken by pages or by children of the nobility. If the first performance were public then it is possible that the actors were recruited from the children of the Chapel Royal. The Chapel was officially part of the royal household and consisted, in the 1590s, of twelve children under the supervision of a chaplain as their master and mentor. As early as Henry VIth's reign the children had become noted for their singing abilities and, by the sixteenth century, achieved fame for their performing talent in Christmas plays. In the 1570s and 1580s they gave plays in an old converted building at Blackfriars and, at Court, are known to have presented Lyly's *Campaspe* (1584) and other of his plays under royal command.

The Elizabethan audience would, doubtless, have delighted in their appearance as fairies in *A Midsummer Night's Dream*; and indeed, on those occasions when modern directors have used children, the result has usually been successful. It is astonishing, however, how comparatively rarely twentieth-century productions have risked the use of children in these parts. In truth, there is little risk. What is required is charming unsophistication, and most children, unless they have been sullied by over-exposure to the publicity which attends modern theatre, are more than capable of achieving this.

We are introduced to the play's three worlds in strict order. First Theseus's court, then the lower orders, followed by Oberon's kingdom. The order is important and, indeed, seems deliberate. The centre of the action is, in fact, the court of Theseus; his marriage has priority and it is right that we should be introduced to this centre at the outset. What occurs at the court gives a hint of darkness to the action—Hermia and Lysander are placed under a threat. Shakespeare has stated the threat simply, yet although anyone accustomed to the conventions of pastoral comedy will know that the threat will be lifted, he makes doubly sure that the atmosphere of comedy is seen to prevail. He therefore follows the court scene with a glimpse of the uninhibited earthiness of the amateur theatricals. The direction of the play is thus established but, more, a pleasing and necessary contrast is achieved between conventional sophistication and unconventional realism. The first fairy scene which follows serves a double purpose. It is, in itself, a piquant reflexion of the earthly world—even Oberon and Titania have their marital problems. It also amplifies the implication of a happy conclusion by involving the possibility of magical intervention.

These three scenes are also remarkable for the fact that there is no sense of sudden and incredible transition from one to another. It seems natural that we should go from Duke to weaver to Fairy King and Queen. This natural flow is achieved in several ways. Firstly, the forest itself is a focal point for the actions of these scenes. We know that the lovers will go to the forest; we arrive there before them and meet the actors, and we remain there to meet the fairies. Second, there is a natural connexion, stated immediately, between the events we have seen in scene one and what we see in the subsequent two scenes. It is right that we should meet the actors for they "are thought fit through all Athens to play in our interlude before the Duke and the Duchess on his wedding day at night". It is equally right that we should meet the fairies and that they should be in this part of the forest, for one of the accusations that Oberon hurls at Titania is this:

> How canst thou thus, for shame, Tytania,
> Glaunce at my credit, with *Hippolita*?
> Knowing I know thy love to *Theseus*.
> [II. I. 74-7]

The situations grows in piquancy as the connexions are established. A marriage has been arranged, entertainments are planned, and the King and Queen of the fairies mutually accuse each other of affections for the mortals. The piquancy is delightful, and it is part of Shakespeare's subtle unifying of the three areas of activity to which we have been severally introduced. There is one other factor which makes for unity. Stanley Wells[8] writes:

> Stress is laid already on the moon, an image whose recurrence will help to create the play's unity of poetic style. It sheds its radiance throughout, lingering Theseus's desires, beholding the night of his solemnities, providing a setting for the meeting of the Fairy King and Queen, quenching Cupid's arrow in its beams, looking with a watery eye upon Titania and Bottom, and making a personal appearance in the interlude of Pyramus and Thisbe.

It is, indeed, idle to search the play for depth of characterisation;

the four lovers are of a piece, with slight variations. They are courtly, well-bred, and reasonably attractive in personality. Helena is created in the mould of the typical rejected maiden of pastoral romance—always within reach of tears. Hermia has more individuality; she has a stronger will, is a little pert, and is always within reach of a tart remark. She has something of Rosalind's independence and a touch of Maria's tongue. Demetrius would sort well with Orlando at his most self-indulgent. He is always within reach of the sighing romantic phrase and he has less spunk than Lysander who knows his mind and heart and will reach for a conclusion with both hands. Hippolyta is almost all mythological—the true Amazon regal beauty, only just tamed—but not quite. She is eventually humanised by Shakespeare when she expresses a feminine irritability with Theseus's patience towards the amateur actors.

Bottom is basically likeable not merely because he is put in a position with his ass's head where we can laugh at him, but simply because his fellows adore him. Without him they are lost; he is the prop and staff of their dithery journey towards the limelight; he is the acknowledged king of their society. When he returns from his strange adventure it is like the return of the prodigal, and it is a total triumph. He has come back to his people who need him.

There are no doubts about Shakespeare's knowledge of amateur theatricals. We are given the nervous prompter, the star, the confuser of cues, the reluctant heroine, the Armaggedon of temperament. Some commentators have seen in Bottom a satirical portrait of the professional actor, with all his self-indulgences. It is possible to accept the feasibility of this while, at the same time, making a qualification. Satire, in its truest sense, involves an element of condemnation, but no condemnation is made of these rough and ready men, nor of their leader. They are presented for us to laugh at, but we leave them with a glow of warmth. The comedy that emerges from their scenes is affirmative in the richest sense of the word—it affirms honest if unaccustomed toil, a desire to please, and a horny-handed kind of dignity.

The theatrical episodes are not mere extracts in a story of romantic and supernatural love; the tender touch which makes all things well for the world of lovers is also present in Bottom's kingdom. He and his fellows become an inextricable part of a happy unity.

If the centre of the plot is the events of Theseus's court, the meaning of the unity which radiates from the plot is implicit in Theseus's character. He uses these phrases:

> everlasting band of fellowshipe.
>
> [I. I. 85]

> Wee will, faire Queene, up to the mountaines toppe
> And marke the musicall confusion
> Of hounds and Echo in conjunction.
>
> [IV. I. 106-8]

> How comes this gentle concord in the worlde,
> That hatred is so farre from jealousie,
> To sleepe by hate and feare no enmitie.
>
> [IV. I. 140-2]

> For never anything can be amisse
> When simplenesse and duety tender it.
>
> [V. I. 83-4]

> Our sport shall be, to take what they mistake
> And what poore duty cannot doe, noble respect
> Takes it in might, not merit.
>
> [V. I. 90-2]

> If we imagine no worse of them, then they of
> themselves, they may passe for excellent men.
>
> [V. I. 212-14]

This man is by way of being a philosopher, but it is no academic way of thought, and it is all bent actively towards one purpose—to achieve a true conjunction of hearts and minds in his domain. He is a true law-giver, and abides by it in saying that Hermia must abide her father's wishes or suffer the penalty. But he is benevolent, and one would like to know what he said to Hermia's father:

> I must employ you in some businesse,
> Against our nuptiall, and conferre with you
> Of some thing nerely that concernes your selves.
>
> [I. I. 124-6]

—we do not know, but it is easy to guess that he is appealing for humanity. He is surprised, but does not argue, when he finds that former enmities have dissipated—he is content when he sees the four lovers lying together, that amity has been achieved. He chides Hippolyta's impatience at what are, for her, the longeurs of the Pyramus and Thisbe play with these words:

> The best, in this kinde, are but shadowes: and the worst are no worse, if imagination amend them.
>
> [II. I. 209-11]

If one were to search for an image which would embody the meaning of Theseus's presence in the play, it would be found in some stage-business in the R.S.T. production of 1961. Bottom, as Pyramus, has given his greatest performance; the entertainment ends; Bottom stands triumphant and flushed. In his ecstasy he drops his ludicrous wooden sword; it lies between him and Theseus. There is a pause. The duke bends, picks it up, lays it in a graceful and chivalrous gesture across his left arm and, with a bow, presents it to Bottom. Their eyes meet for a moment. In that moment there is a "gentle concord in the world". Class, status, even occasion is forgotten—two people have met and they understand that nothing can be amiss; it is a kind of loving. If there is one generalisation, which few would deny, about Shakespeare's dramatic work, it is that it was written by a man who had a detestation of disorder and chaos and a consequent obsession for bringing together dissident people and attitudes. "Only connect" is a useful phrase to describe what seems to be Shakespeare's personal aspiration for mankind.

From time to time in the plays, this aspiration is specifically embodied in characters who, in varying degrees, seem to see more, understand more, than is seen or understood by those around them. The Duke in *Measure for Measure* is such a man,

Ulysses (explicitly lauding the virtues of order) is another. Prospero, above all, fits the category so closely that there have been persistent attempts to identify the character with Shakespeare himself—as if the image finally merged with reality. To an extent Theseus comes into this company. He embodies, and makes more explicit, the play's drive towards a sense of unity and reconciliation. His mind is open to be convinced and persuaded—to this extent he is rational man. He gives the impression of possessing a wisdom denied to others—to this extent he is a civilised man. He is a kind of statesman of the human heart and his "philosophical" comments, his stern but fair conception of legality, and his treatment of the mechanicals all underline the play's quest for a happy unity. Because of Theseus the play's meaning is absolutely clear. Human happiness can only be achieved by a constant vigilance by human beings to see that their imaginations and intelligences are open, charitably, towards others. In order to sustain this, man must accept others for what they are, not for what they might be. The lovers learn that to achieve happiness they need mutual understanding and tolerance; the mechanicals achieve their heart's desire—to be successful before their Duke, and they are successful because he is willing to accept them for the goodness of their intentions.

The transfiguration of all concerned is completed in the last scene where the house and its occupants are blessed by the fairy world. Oberon's speech is a celebration of concord:

> Now untill the breake of day,
> Through this house, each Fairy stray.
> To the best bride bed will wee:
> Which by us shall blessed be;
> And the issue, there create,
> Ever shall be fortunate:
> So shall all the couples three
> Ever true in loving be:
> And the blots of natures hand
> Shall not in their issue stand.
>
> [v. i. 390–9]

The language of the play is an emblem of its aspiration for concord out of disparate matters. It is useless to search for a single style in the play, and yet the final impression is that a single style is present. The word "lyrical" covers a multitude of effects—both laudable and unworthy—and it has been employed over and over again to describe the language. The truth is, that so potent is the play's drive towards concord, that we believe its language to be all of a piece—a kind of rhythmic singing. This is not so. Bottom speaks:

> I have had a most rare vision. I have had a dreame,
> past the wit of man, to say what dreame it was.
> Man is but an Asse, if hee goe about to expound this dreame.
> Me thought I was, there is no man can tell what. Me thought
> I was, and me thought I had. But man is but patcht a foole,
> if hee will offer to say what mee thought I had.
>
> [IV. I. 201-9]

Puck speaks

> I am that merry wanderer of the night.
> I jest to *Oberon*, and make him smile
> When I a fat and beane-fed horse beguile;
> Neyghing, in likenesse of a filly fole.
>
> [II. I. 43-6]

Hermia speaks:

> *Lysander* riddles very prettily.
> Now much beshrewe my manners, and my pride,
> If *Hermia* meant to say, *Lysander* lyed.
> But gentle friend, for love and courtesie,
> Ly further off, in humane modesty:
> Such separation, as may well be said
> Becomes a vertuous bacheler, and a maide,
> So farre be distant, and good night, sweete friend;
> Thy love nere alter till thy sweete life end.
>
> [II. II. 53-61]

And Oberon speaks:

> My gentle *Pucke* come hither: Thou remembrest,
> Since once I sat upon a promontory,
> And heard a Mearemaid, on a Dolphins backe,
> Uttering such dulcet and harmonious breath,
> That the rude sea grewe civill at her song,
> And certaine starres shot madly from their spheares,
> To heare the Sea-maids musick.
>
> [II. I. 148-54]

The superficial pattern of each speech is easily stated. Bottom's prose invokes the unflighted prosaicness of his mind and status; Puck's tinkling rhyme embodies the staccato magic of his existence; Hermia's insistent and mechanical liturgy bespeaks the conventional behaviour of the modest romantic heroine; Oberon's high and wide-ranging music takes us out of time, and charms us to accept the magic world. All these are examples of the amazing variety of style in the language of the play. What gives us the sense of one style is the theme itself and the insistent charm of the language, whatever form it may take in different speakers. The charm consists of one basic element—a patina of happy optimism which informs the communication of the play. In the long run *A Midsummer Night's Dream* is Shakespeare's happiest play, and it is tempting to believe that it is so partly because it was written at a time when his career was beginning to glow with success.

From begin to end it the idea of death is foreshadowed

4

TRAGEDY AND TRAGI-COMEDY

1. *Romeo and Juliet*

Romeo and Juliet is commonly accepted by audiences as one of Shakespeare's most affecting tragedies. Its popularity is easily explained—it is a tragedy of love. Romantic love, whether it be in the comic or tragic mode, is a constant attraction to the playgoer. The theme of this play which relates the defiance, by two young people, of accepted conventions of behaviour and of an unexplained animosity between their elders, makes a direct appeal to the natural human desire to break out of the constrictions built up by centuries of accepted behaviour. It matters little to audiences whether, in plays of romantic love, the relationship between the lovers is finally accepted (a comic affirmation) or if it be consummated only to be finally broken (the tragic pathos); the actual process of love and loving under conditions of stress and opposition induces a strong sense of identification between the audience and the fictional participants. The comic version produces a state of happy nostalgia for personal opportunities that may not have been taken; the tragic version raises up the pathetic feeling: "There, but for the grace of God, go I."

Romantic tragedy, in particular, incites identification because, basically, its ingredients can be easily correlated with basic human imaginative experience. Love is celebrated (certainly in this play) through words which are worthy of the subject but, more important, those words give expression to passions which are common to human experience; it expresses what most have felt but have found inexpressible. Moreover it catches the heart of love at that time of life when its effects are felt most keenly.

D

Adolescent love is self-indulgent, reckless and, to the onlooker, frequently poignant. Those who experience it (and that is the majority of people) find it totally absorbing, and any bar to its full expression overwhelmingly great and unbearable. It is experienced at such a pitch of involvement that both its joys and despairs are immense—one kiss describes eternal joy, one slight signals total disaster.

Romeo and Juliet reflects all this but it carries the matter one stage further than most human experience. In this play the odds against young love are too high; what is a melodramatic possibility becomes a reality and these two lovers become, for the sympathetic beholder, sacrifices whose memories are constantly to be worshipped.

Despite, perhaps because of, the doom which descends upon Romeo and Juliet, the very intensity of their discovering each other is an affirmation of love itself:

> Though lovers be lost, love shall not,
> And Death shall have no dominion.[1]

Romantic tragedy is, therefore, tragedy of a very particular kind— of and for youth. The play's special affiliations with youth, nostalgia, and verbal beauty must be kept in mind when its tragic qualities are considered.

Quite obviously the play cannot be accepted as fulfilling the kind of expectation we have from Shakespeare's four major plays in this mode. Those plays teach us, as indeed do classical Greek tragedies, to associate the highest tragic experience with the working out of the destiny of one dominant male protagonist. This play has no dominant male hero; it does not, in either of its main characters, show the presence of a flaw in personality which is played upon to incite the final catastrophe; again, although Fate is present, it emerges too mechanistically—the catastrophe seems less inevitable than avoidable. In these respects particularly, the play fails to measure up to what is tacitly accepted as the ultimate tragic experience as it is presented in Shakespeare's major tragedies. Of these ingredients, the existence and status of a major male protagonist is of most vital importance. The loneliness, the fight against fate, the descent towards ruin—these are the factors which, above all, create the fabric of great tragedy. Romeo and Juliet share a destiny; although they die they are, in our minds, like Juliet's beauty, not conquered. They lie forever together in a silent but total love. Tragic tension is, as it were, divided *because* they are allowed to share eternity with each other. They lose, in being together, the final crown of loneliness which, in the great tragic protagonists, makes them, at one and the same time, pitiably small and defiantly large. It has often been said that Mercutio's virile presence in the play is necessarily cut short by Shakespeare since his vivacity and realism of outlook threatens any sympathies we may have for Romeo. What is most striking about Mercutio is, however, the effect of his death upon us in the audience. It strikes more shockingly into our hearts than does that of the two lovers. Theirs gives us a long regret, his wounds with savage intensity. More to the point, their death is romantically logistical, his seems an ironic waste. Without, obviously, being a tragic protagonist, in the sense in which we think of Hamlet, there is a sense in which the effect of his death upon us can be compared with that of Hamlet. He is established as a credible, active personality (more so, at first, than Romeo), but, most important, there is a curious quality of isolation about him. He is a loner. It becomes fitting, in the end, that Romeo and Juliet should die together; it is altogether unfitting that Mercutio should die. His departure is nearer the high tragic status which involves irony and a sense of waste, and he and he alone takes us anywhere near those frontiers beyond which lie the immensities of tragic experience of Lear and Hamlet.

The actual plot is derived from a poem by Arthur Brooke— *The Tragicall Historye of Romeus and Juliet*—which appeared in 1562. Brooke's poem was, however, only one version of the very popular basic story of the love and death of two young lovers which is found in many forms, particularly in Italy in the fifteenth and sixteenth centuries.[2] Shakespeare may have known other versions, including a lost play to which Brooke refers in the preface to his poem, but this cannot be taken for granted. The important point is that the basic story was immensely popular and well-known and that many of the versions have certain common denominators. The operations of fate, the opposition of parents, the effects of the stars on the lovers—these are some of the abiding features of the story. The romantic cast of Shakespeare's play is, indeed, an indigenous part of the basic story. It must be stressed, however, that the play shows three particular qualities which are exclusive to Shakespeare himself. The first may be readily understood when it is recalled that the play is the first tragedy he wrote after the early and immature *Titus Andronicus*. There is much in the play to show that he had not yet freed himself from the influence of the Senecan mode of tragedy which that early play displays with such lack of inhibition. The general air of violence about to break out, the bloodshed, the scene in the graveyard and the emphasis on Tybalt in his bloody shroud—all these derive from the Roman dramatist.

The second is the evidence of Shakespeare's dramatic skill. Brooke makes the action last over several months; Shakespeare reduces it to a few days and increases the tragic poignancy of the events; Brooke leans heavily towards moralising, making the tale into an awful warning to youth against promiscuity and parental disobedience. Shakespeare avoids an explicit didacticism, being more concerned with the human reality of the events; Brooke's Juliet is a flighty miss, revelling in her deception of her mother; Shakespeare's Juliet is vulnerable, unsophisticated, and torn between the duties of love and of parental affection.

The third is the language of the play. Its distinctiveness lies not only in its intrinsic qualities but in what it foreshadows. On the one hand it is undoubtedly written in the same key as the language of the sonnets, where metaphor, simile, conceit, are used at a high degree of lyric intensity. On the other hand it shows evidences of a more dramatic use of language where what is said, its imagery, and the speaking character, are closely integrated. The first, more highly wrought and lyrical speech, is evidenced in Romeo and Juliet's first meeting, the second in Mercutio's language—with the exception of the speech to Queen Mab.

On a superficial view the play might be regarded as a dramatised poem—a lyric exploration of young love doomed by circumstance and the operations of malevolent stars. This view runs the danger of neglecting its skilful dramatic force which deepens and widens our experience of the events. The play, indeed, does not have the emotional simplicities which we know from operatic treatment. It holds, within itself, one large tension from which certain complexities radiate. This tension is well described by T. J. B. Spencer:[3] "There are constant and deliberate collisions between romantic and unromantic views of love".

The play contains two worlds—that which Romeo and Juliet inhabit, and that of all the rest of the characters. The lovers' world attempts to be self-sufficient, nourished solely by the power of love. It is based on the pathetic fallacy that to love is enough. It admits of actions which are precipitately undertaken. Its absorption in itself makes its feelings sensitive and liable to loss of control:

> Oh tell me Frier tell me,
> In what vile part of this Anatomie
> Doth my name lodge? Tell me, that I may sacke
> The hatefull mansion.
>
> [III. III. 105-8]

It is Romeo, more than Juliet, who convinces us that theirs is a world which is attempting to insulate itself from any intrusion. In the course of the action he moves from a position which is based entirely upon an unreal and melodramatic notion of love for Rosalind to a real, passionate, and all-absorbing love for Juliet. Indeed, when we first meet him, he is already insulated from outside communication and his solitary self-indulgence is not only implicit in his speech but in the comments of others:

> But to himselfe so secret and so close.
>
> [I. I. 147]

His love for Juliet only drives him further into a situation where the outside world seems to him an irrelevance, an irritant and a danger:

> Unless Philosophie can make a *Juliet*,
> Displant a towne, reverse a Princes doome,
> It helpes not, prevailes not, talke no more.
>   [III. III. 58-60]

Although his realisation of his love for Juliet makes him, for a short time, more capable of consorting with the jests and quips of his fellows, giving them good answer, it is not long before he enters again the other world. The irritation that lurks beneath our experience of his character in the theatre derives from this simple fact that, except briefly, he seems incapable of making any real concession to the realities of the everyday world. Juliet has more of our sympathy for we have the impression that, despite her youthfulness, there is a greater practicality in her nature. We get the sense that any attempt by Romeo to ease his haste would find a response from her. She is a more attractive character because she seems to be conscious of other duties which lie outside a total indulgence to love. She knows her duties to her parents; she is agonisingly aware of the different but powerful love that she bears for her kinsman, Tybalt. It is only towards the end of the play that Romeo shows a deeper sensibility about the existence of others. His reaction to Mercutio's death certainly has about it a reckless courage, but our admiration for his quick response is tempered by the curiously effete mentality which shows itself in the weak line in reply to Mercutio's question about why he came between him and Tybalt. Romeo says:

> I thought all for the best.

In a sense we find it difficult to trust the emotional spirit of Romeo. At no point in the play can we be sure that he is not being governed by passions whose consequence has never been considered by him. Juliet seems a more complete and reliable person, despite her youth. She engages our sympathies for this, and also because she is shown to be taking the greatest personal risk in deciding to take the Friar's potion. It is because Juliet seems to have a more outgoing sensibility than Romeo, and is more sensitive to outside factors, that the insulation which the two lovers try to coil about them seems poignant and vulnerable.

The outside world is depicted with equal force. The lovers are shown to be besieged from several sides, and each of them is sharply designated. The first scene of the play, for example, shows the restless, niggling, and potentially dangerous condition of the Capulet/Montague feud; this is exaggerated by the presence of Tybalt. He is, in fact, the active element in a feud which, for the most part, rumbles distantly and always seems about to break out into bloodshed. Shakespeare personalises, and therefore heightens, the meaning of the feud by means of this character— a spoilt darling of a noble family. He represents one of the chief dangers which beleaguers the lovers, but the representation is given sharper focus because of Tybalt's relationship to Juliet.

Within the general context of the feud yet another more precise enemy to the lovers is embedded and, yet again, Shakespeare personalises it. Children, particularly daughters, must abide the wishes and edicts of their fathers, especially in the matter of marriage. Whatever sympathies the Elizabethan audience had for Juliet, these would have been tempered by the plain knowledge that she was disobeying a law which, to them, was natural. What is remarkable, however, about the depiction of the dis- obedience, is the dramatic quality of the personal clash between Juliet and her father. Capulet is a superb study of a small-minded, well-meaning man accustomed, because of his wealth and position, to getting his own way. Shakespeare has understood the psychology of such men perfectly. They are prepared to show *bonhommie* in situations where they feel relaxed, in control, and the centre of attention. Capulet is prepared even to accept Romeo at his banquet:

> I would not for the wealth of all this Towne,
> Here in my house do him disparagement.
>
> [I. v. 67-8]

He can afford, as the only begetter of the feast, to show what, under the circumstances, is a very temporary magnanimity. Yet the narrowness of his sensibilities is exposed in his tirade to Juliet when she begs not to be forced to marry Paris:

> Hang thee, young baggage! Disobedient wretch!
> I tell thee what—get thee to church a' Thursday
> Or never after look me in the face.
>
> [III. V. 160-62]

Capulet's world is a fundamentally crude and cruel place. It has many adherents, and its strongest citizen (and the lovers' most insidious enemy) is the Nurse.

She is a woman for all seasons; she hunts with the hounds and runs with the hares. She is Shakespeare's most effective study in fickleness, and she is all the more impressive a dramatic creation because she plays a dual role. On one level she is lined up on the side of the outside world. Her bawdiness, her basic crudity of sense and sensibility, seem like a sore against the white flesh of Romeo and Juliet's love. To her, love means sex, marriage means bed, and the swelling female belly the only possible affirmation of the existence of love. Yet she is more than a mere repository of all that is opposite to the delicate lyrical world of the two lovers. She is their enemy in a more subtle, and certainly more dramatically telling sense. It is, after all, only by her lumbering and creaking help that the lovers are able to come together—she becomes a conspirator on their behalf. She is the only female that Juliet can turn to to share her excited joy in her new-found love—to this extent she becomes the child's confessor. Both Romeo and Juliet, but particularly the latter, accept her as a natural ally. The blow to Juliet when the Nurse, falling ponderously in step with the establishment she is bound to serve, denounces Romeo, is great and painful. She tells the girl that one man is as good as another—her philosophy of expediency strikes at the very heart of the consuming love Juliet bears for Romeo. She blows a chill wind into a world which is all warmth and youth:

> I thinke you are happie in this second match,
> For it excels your first.
>
> [III. V. 223-4]

The nurse's treachery has the effect not only of increasing our feeling that the lovers are gradually being isolated, but also of isolating Juliet herself who, unlike Romeo, has striven to maintain some commerce with her family. Our sympathy for Juliet is increased and given an added dimension by the cold anxiety which strikes us as she prepares to take the potion. But, more than this, the Nurse's words, and Juliet's reactions to them, matures her presence and gives her a brave resolve to proceed in her course, alone if necessary:

> Thou and my bosome henceforth shall be twaine.
>
> [III. v. 241]

It is largely because of the Nurse that Juliet is confirmed as having much the stronger character of the two lovers.

Yet this nurse exists in the play on another level—one more attractive and dramatically direct. Shakespeare has unerringly created a picture of an old family retainer—almost a type. Limited in intelligence, proud in her status, the recipient of family confidences, emotionally unstable—so that tears fall as readily as laughter. This type, which has since become familiar to us in countless novels and plays, is a kind of chameleon, taking its colouring from the safest atmosphere it can find. The Nurse is Mistress Quickly domesticated, and she endears herself to us less for her actual characteristics than for the perceptible limitations of those characteristics. The Nurse, and Quickly, lack taste in everything; their laughter is always overdone; their sentimentality is always slightly misplaced; their judgment is non-existent; their anger is unblessed with rational excuse; their fidelity is confined to the proposition that they serve best he who pays the piper.

The insidious intrusion of the outside world is thus clearly expressed through the medium of several characters. There is one, however, who stands between both worlds and attempts to reconcile them. The traditional way of playing Friar Laurence emphasises a kind of holy ineffectiveness and reduces him to an effete and wordy fool. Granville-Barker[4] refers to him as "poor Friar Laurence" and as "deplorable" as a man of affairs. He claims that his reproof to the lovers is "near to cant". Recently, T. J. B. Spencer,[5] showing less dismissiveness, is still inclined to disparage the man. He is "well-meaning, kindly, good-humoured". The majority of actors, in twentieth-century productions, concentrate their interpretations on superfluous simplicity. Yet this Friar occupies a vitally important position in the play.

His first speech, when he is discovered collecting herbs, is often accepted by actors and directors as a testimony to the verbose ineffectuality of the man but, in fact, it is a reflexion of some of the themes which are developed in the play's action. Romeo and Juliet's precipitate action is defined in the words:

> Vertue it selfe turnes vice being misapplied.
>
> [II. III. 21]

The situation in the city is mirrored in the lines:

> Two such opposed Kings encamp them still,
> In man as well as hearbes, grace and rude will.
>
> [II. III. 27-8]

and Spencer admits that the speech prepares us for the Friar's preparation of the potion which Juliet takes and for the poison which Romeo buys. The Friar is not a remote eremite. He is far more precise and direct about Romeo's state of mind than even Mercutio:

> . . . Young men's love then lies
> Not truly in their hearts, but in their eies.
> Jesu *Maria*, what a deale of brine
> Hath washt thy sallow cheekes for *Rosaline*?
> How much salt water throwne away in waste,
> To season love, that of it doth not taste.
>
> [II. III. 67-72]

He is well aware, long before the crisis initiated by Tybalt's death, of the dangers that Romeo invites.

> Wisely and slow, they stumble that run fast.
>
> [II. III. 94]

He is purposeful in committing himself to helping the two lovers, though the consequences are clear to him:

> So smile the heavens upon this holy act,
> That after houres, with sorrow chide us not.
>
> [II. VI. 1-2]

His strictures on Romeo when he arrives after killing Tybalt
are, far from being "cant", a model of righteous anger, followed
by practical advice. It is noticeable that his words to Romeo for
the greater part of the scene are delivered in short clear sentences.
He does not sermonise to this blubbering young man, but is
unequivocal in what he says:

> I bring thee tidings of the Princes doome.
>
> [III. III. 8]

> Here from *Verona* art thou banished:
> Be patient, for the world is broad and wide.
>
> [III. III. 15-16]

> O, then I see, that mad men have no eares.
>
> [III. III. 61]

When he does essay a long speech in this scene, it is not cant that
comes but a passionately rational series of points. It is altogether
correct, psychologically, that he should, at the end of the scene,
make a long speech, since Romeo has just attempted to stab
himself, and what he needs at this point are exactly the home
truths that the Friar hurls at him. He is no less direct and practical
when Juliet visits him after being told, to her despair, that she
must marry Paris.

In personality, then, he is far from ineffective and simple.
He helps the lovers; his advice, under the circumstances, is
rational, and he cannot be blamed that events turn all his well-
made plans awry. This Friar, standing between two worlds,
represents, in his function, what the ideal solution would have
been—an acceptance of the inevitability of the love of the two
young people and its legal sanction. His humanity enables him to
accept their love, his profession urges him to legalise what he has,
as human being, already accepted. It is no fault of his that a solution
is impossible—he cannot control their precipitancy, and he has
no legislation over ill-crossed stars and intransigent parents.

Shakespeare ~~is more~~ precise (indeed uncharacteristically so) in this play about giving the audience time-checks on the duration of the dramatic action than in any other play. The events begin on a Sunday morning and end in the early morning of the following Thursday. They take place in high summer. At many points along the play's action time-signposts are given. Romeo appears soon after nine on Sunday morning; the lovers meet that evening, their conversation takes place about midnight on that evening. At nine on Monday morning Romeo is at Friar Laurence's cell, marries Juliet that afternoon, and kills Tybalt about an hour later. The lovers part at dawn on Tuesday morning and, on the same day, Juliet gets the potion from Friar Laurence. On Wednesday morning Juliet is discovered, apparently dead. Romeo arrives at the tomb in the early hours of Thursday morning.

All these details are expressly given, or unequivocally implied, in the text, and often with such emphasis as to leave no doubt that Shakespeare was at pains to ensure that his audience knew where it was on the time-scale:

> CAP: But soft, what day is this?
> PARIS: Monday my Lord.
> CAP: Monday, ha, ha, well wendsday is too soone,
>   A thursday let it be, a thursday tell her.
>   [III. IV. 18–20]

The effect of this knowledge is to give a sense of precipitancy which achieves an immediate boost by the bringing forward of Juliet's proposed marriage by one day—from Thursday to Wednesday:

> LADY CAP: No, not till Thursday, there is time inough.
> CAP: Go, Nurse, go with her, weele to Church
>   to morrow.
>   [IV. II. 36–7]

The sense of haste is increased, in a naturalistic way, by the frequent references of the Friar to the dangers of haste, and his head-shaking doubts about it, and it is further emphasised by the skilful juxtapositions of the temperaments of the leading

characters with the chronological time-scheme. The first scene
of the play with its sense of quick danger, the volatile Mercutio
jumping from thought to thought, the itchy sword-fingers and
abrasive temper of Tybalt—all these conspire with the play's
clock-time to give a sense of onrush. The text gives the stage-
director a deal of opportunity to reinforce the sense of speed.
The first scene, and that in which Mercutio taunts Tybalt, take
place in the hot July Italian sun. There is a telling paradox,
particularly in the second example, that such swift action should
take place at a time which is traditionally siesta. In Franco
Zeffirelli's production at the Old Vic[6] this paradox was emphasised
so that, in scene one, there was an impression both of danger and
pointlessness in the feud and, in the other scene, the poignancy of
Mercutio's death was increased by its taking place in hot sunlight
—a context for living not dying.

The naturalistic evocations of time moving quickly and of
actions and people keeping pace with it is paralleled by the
imagery by which Romeo in particular and Juliet, to a less extent,
express themselves about life and love:

> Too like the lightning which doth cease to bee,
> Ere one can say, it lightens.
>
> [II. II. 119-20]
>
> A lightning before death.
>
> [V. III. 90]
>
> . . . too rash, too unadvisd, too sudden.
>
> [II. II. 118]

Both lovers show a consciousness of what their love is bound by,
and both see it as a swift incandescence. One part of their minds
and feelings, which sees their love thus, moves even faster than
the relentless clock-time which dictates the speed of the action
that surrounds them.

Yet Shakespeare's most conspicuous triumph is his ability to
make the clock-face of the action transparent, as it were. Other
time-scales, and consequently other values, can be perceived, and,
in our perception of them, a poignant irony enters into our
experience of the whole action.

In the first place, there is the ruminative time-scale which the Nurse reveals and, to an extent, Capulet. She is given to journeying, in a mumbling way, into the past: "I remember it well", "I never shall forget it". Capulet, with the nostalgia of an elderly man feeling the neural itch of youth, is given also to slow remembrance: "I have seen the day", "'Tis gone, 'tis gone, 'tis gone". The effect of this time-scale is to provide a pathetic contrast to the actual time the lovers have at their disposal. As Spencer says: "The four days are framed, as it were, by many years". It may also be suggested that the implied contrast also suggests the denial of the possibility of two lovers' growing into old age together.

In the second place, there is the implicit time-scale which exists as a kind of wry aspiration in the two lovers. Their conscious minds tell them that their love is a thing of lightning, their desires force them to indulge in the pathetic fallacy that the lightning flash is, indeed, eternal in duration. They attempt to annihilate the temporary at several points. Their imagery tries, from time to time, to identify their mutual love with something other than the lightning flash. For Romeo, Juliet's beauty is often identified with eternal verities:

> The brightnesse of her cheek would shame the stars.
>
> [II. II. 19]

and she is "as a winged messenger of heaven". Even at the end "Bewtie's ensigne yet is crymson in thy lips and in thy cheeks"; he thinks she is dead but, for him, she has conquered death.

Juliet is no less apt in this process:

> My bountie is as boundlesse as the sea,
> My love as deepe, The more I give to thee,
> The more I have, for both are infinite.
>
> [II. II. 133-5]

For Romeo, when Juliet is present, "Heaven is here", and he, echoing another man who tried to seek immortality out of swift mortality, and conjured up Helen for the purpose, talks of "the immortal blessing from Juliet's lips". On their wedding-night the fallacy of this attempt to defy the facts of time come to the surface. They are both prepared to deny the natural evidence of clock-time, even to sacrifice themselves on behalf of the sweet counter-feiting they indulge in:

> Ile say yon grey is not the mornings eye.
> [III. v. 19]

The language and imagery enable the audience to see through the clock-face to the heart of the reality of Romeo and Juliet's experience of love. This is no more starkly experienced than in the scene of Capulet's banquet, which seems to exist simultaneously in two different time-scales. There is the bustling present tense, with its reminders of normal chronology, in Capulet's references to the past, his conversation with his cousin about age, in Tybalt's fierce reactions to Romeo's presence, in Capulet's remark about the lateness of the hour—"It waxes late". Within this undecoratedly expressed present tense there lies the exquisitely lyrical timeless moment of Romeo and Juliet's first meeting. The audience is almost jolted from one time-scale to another by the contrast in the language-patterns. Tybalt's words:

> I will withdraw, but this intrusion shall,
> Now seeming sweet, convert to bittrest gall.
> [I. v. 89-90]

are followed by:

> If I profane with my unworthiest hand
> This holy shrine, the gentle sin is this.
> [I. v. 91-2]

and the gentle and kissed farewell of the two lovers is followed by a raucous return to the present tense in the Nurse's shout:

> Madam your mother craves a word with you.
> [I. v. 109]

The different time-values of this scene are definitely indicated by the contrasting language-patterns of the two worlds which are brought into existence in the banquet. No more striking confirmation of the contrast and its effects could be imagined than in Franco Zeffirelli's production of the scene. The restless present tense was depicted in bustling movement, gay dancing, laughter, and loud music at back-stage. Out of this the two lovers emerged to meet front-stage. At the moment of recognition of love and beauty, both the visual and aural impression of the present tense began to fade and, as the love-dialogue between the two developed, the present-tense action in the background was deliberately slowed down—coming almost to a stop. The impression was as if a timeless moment had been created and had begun to dominate the present tense—almost to the point of annihilating it.

Romeo and Juliet pathetically aspire for a perpetuation of this moment; their tragedy is that their aspiration is impossible.

Yet the play's whole movement is dominated by inevitability. It does not really allow of a change of direction in the resolution of the action, so surrounded is it with a sense of malevolent fate. Destiny is an utterly dominant dramatis persona in the play; its presence is announced by the chorus, by Romeo, Juliet, and the Friar. The Elizabethan audience would have paid more attention to the operations of Fate than do we, although it must be allowed that there is still more than a lingering addiction to astrology in English audiences. It was, however, completely natural to take notice of the configurations of the stars and to make, and believe in, predictions.

The play's main weakness is that its insistence upon the malevolent stars to produce an inevitable result is at variance with the mechanics of the plot-line. One part of us will say that the outcome is inevitable, but another cannot help reflecting that a mere slight turn in the mechanics of the plot could change the conclusion. This weakness is a measure of Shakespeare's relative immaturity in the face of one of the first tragedies he attempted to write which was attempting more than the mechanical horrifics of Seneca. When the play is measured against the great tragedies in which fate, human will and choice are in exact tension, this play seems deficient. Yet this is an example where the sheer force of lyrical beauty, theatrical movement and that indefinable attraction which lures us to identify something in us with what happens to young love, overrides the results of comparing it with greater plays.

2. *The Merchant of Venice*

This play, written between 1596 and 1598[7], is one of the most popular in the whole canon. The first quarto records that it was "diuers times" performed by the Lord Chamberlain's company (possibly with Burbage playing Shylock). In the eighteenth century Betterton played Bassanio and a well-known comic actor (John Downes) played Shylock. In 1741 Macklin rejected the comic vein and created a villainous criminal from the part. He played it, to great acclaim, on twenty-two occasions. Kemble played Shylock intermittently between 1784 and 1804, with Sarah Siddons as Portia. Kean followed, interpreting the Jew as a man as much sinned against as sinning, and Macready followed him, continuing the rehabilitation into something sympathetic to the audience. Henry Irving's performance represents the culmination of the process that took Shylock from comic to villain to noble proud victim of a vindictive society. In the twentieth century it is the noble Jew that has dominated the innumerable versions of the part that have been presented.

Appraisal of the play is difficult since the experience of it, either in the study or in the theatre, is likely, more than with most others, to be conditioned by strong personal predispositions. These include such considerations as: Is the reader, or member of the audience, Christian or Jew? What is one's attitude, if one is both or neither, to the Jews, or, in other words, how far does racialism (a pregnant consideration nowadays) affect one's experience of the play? What is one's attitude to usury? For the, perhaps rare, reader or viewer of the play who, by some process, is able to submerge these considerations, there still remains a factor which is likely to colour his view of the play. It is a literary rather than a social religious or racialist matter though, doubtless, these play some part in it. It is simply that some find the play inherently cynical because the tone of one element in it fits ill with the tone of the other. It is perhaps naïve to state that the romantic resolutions of Belmont are hard to swallow after the stern judgments of the trial scene; or, indeed, to hold that if this is so it may be an implied condemnation of Shakespeare's inability to reconcile what is dramatically irreconcilable. The point may be expressed differently and put in the form of a question: "Is it not possible that Shylock is built too large and too powerful a character to suffer the cheeseparing actions which virtually annihilate him, and this at the hands of characters who lack the depth, understanding and richness of human perception which has been expended on the Jew?" Ten Brinck writing in 1895 had no doubts about this:

> But it is not merely poetic justice that our feelings demand. Shylock has come too close to us, we have learned to know too intimately the grounds of his hatred, of the intensity of his resentment, his figure has become too humanly significant, and the misfortune which overtakes him appeals too deeply to our sympathies, to permit us to be reconciled to the idea that his fate, which moves us tragically, should be conceived otherwise than as a tragedy.[8]

The play bristles with problems involving interpretation, and the nature of the response we are expected to make to it. These problems are reflected in the extraordinary diverse critical responses that it has induced over the years. In 1896 Georg Brandes writing of the play as bringing us to the threshold of a period in Shakespeare's life "instinct with high-pitched gaiety and gladness" adds that "His poetry, his whole existence, now seems to be given over to music, to harmony".[9] In 1927 E. E. Stoll uttered the warning that "The time is past for speaking of Shakespeare as utterly impartial or inscrutable".[10] Yet in 1962 Dover Wilson was as certain that Shakespeare "is neither for nor against Shylock. Shakespeare never takes sides."[11] Whereas Frank Kermode in 1961, having written that the play is "'About' judgment, redemption and mercy"[12] and that "only by a determined effort to avoid the obvious can one mistake the theme of

The Merchant of Venice", John Russell Brown had earlier assured us that "Shakespeare does not enforce a moral in this play—his judgement is implicit only".[13]

It is obvious that the play is capable of engaging us in many ways, but an examination of the many critical responses suggests that it is within the areas of two basic themes that the variations of response and judgment occur. The first is succinctly described by John Russell Brown:

> Shakespeare was so deeply concerned with the ideal of love's wealth in *The Merchant of Venice* that we may presume that it was fundamental to his thinking and feeling about human relationships.[14]

In this context, Portia is presented to us in such a way as to reconcile us to the otherwise unattractive means by which love's wealth is achieved by some of the other characters. Bassanio has more than a touch of extravagant fecklessness about him. Although he chooses the right casket for the most estimably expressed reasons, the speech of acceptance does not square with the impression of the character which we have; it seems a set speech ministering more perhaps to Shakespeare's own preoccupation with the ideal of love's wealth than to the reality of character. Jessica's ungenerous (to say the least) actions are hardly counterbalanced by what we well know about her father's character. Lorenzo seems to fall "for" rather than be in love "with" Nerissa —his taking of her has the smack of delighted convenience. Portia alone gives a sense of the wealth of love. She, like Perdita and Rosalind, has a total generosity of spirit and, through this, she alone creates a sense of the wealth of love. Her beauty, her honesty, her fidelity and intelligence but, above all, a grave wisdom about the meaning of the depth of real love, radiates through the others, and, as it were, sanctifies what very much needs to be sanctified:

> I never did repent for dooing good,
> Nor shall not now; for in companions
> That do converse and wast the time together,
> Whose soules doe beare an egall yoke of love,

> There must be needes a like proportion
> Of lyniaments, of manners, and of spirit.
>
> [III. IV. 10-15]

It is important to stress that this gravity of spirit which she shows
rests in its quality rather than in its appearance. There has been
a tradition for actresses to play Portia in their maturer years, and
to create an impression of a woman of the world who has long
awaited marriage and, in the interim, devoted herself to an
assiduous study of the law. She is often dressed maturely, and
delivers her speeches with a kind of judicial and elderly sincerity.
The Portia whose task is to irradiate the spirit of love's true
wealth in this play cannot be anything else but young. Her
qualities are, like Rosalind's and Perdita's, natural not acquired.
For them to seem acquired, as they often are depicted, is to
loosen her ability to reconcile us to the love-theme in the pay.
The text supports youth not maturity, not least in the youthful
gamesome spirit evoked in the scene when she and Nerissa
excitedly decide to put on men's attire.

The other basic theme of the play is expressed best by W.
Moelwyn Merchant when he writes:

> We accept the seriousness and technical gravity of the trial
> scene, whatever doubts the juristic side of our minds may
> plead; we respond gravely to the nature of usury and to
> the contrasts of charity, compassion and equity.[15]

He goes on to show how the intertwinings of legal and theo-
logical niceties and the moral questioning which are engendered
by the confrontation of legal quibbling and the idea of charity,
mercy and compassion, are made. Such confrontations are
embedded within the stern framework of opposition between
Christian and Jewish attitudes towards each other, and towards
the quibbles and niceties. These confrontations are not simple—
the mercy expected from the Jew is not seen to be given to him
by the Christians when their turn comes to show it. Again the
differing attitudes of Christian and Jew towards usury where the
one, in Antonio, abhors the practice and the other supports it,

are not shown as a simple black and white contrast. If, in his attitude to it, Antonio seems a plain dealer and Shylock a double dealer, the matter does not rest there. The former has a naïve streak in him, a holier-than-thou satisfaction which hands off our sympathy, while the latter has a persuasive if defensive and fierce loyalty to religious principles which cannot but, at the least, create grudging approval.

It would, therefore, be ludicrous to deny that the play is capable of communication to an audience on a richly speculative level, in terms of these themes which Merchant and Brown have so penetratingly examined. Yet, when all allowance has been made for the existence and subtlety of their appearance, an X factor in the play's quality seems to be missing.

We may approach some conception of this factor by recalling Professor Merchant's words: "The whole legal structure of the play is, of course, fallacious". This is decidedly true. As he points out: "No system of law permits a man to place his own person in jeopardy" and "The impossible change of plea, the exchange of plaintiff and defendant, the intervention of Portia, these all confound strict principles."

The point to hold in mind, while accepting the richness of the play's themes, is one which is suggested by the word "fallacious". The play is popular with audiences of all ages, but most particularly and significantly, with children. It may be doubted whether the majority of audiences "respond gravely" (in Merchant's words) to the themes as expressed by Merchant and Brown, yet they do respond, and enthusiastically, to something.

If the structure of the play is examined carefully it can be shown that there are indications of a careful design on Shakespeare's part to maintain a strong sense of that kind of narrative plot that we associate with the intriguing and the unknown. Quite simply, the play puts its audience, on many occasions, in the position when they ask themselves—what will happen next? This general question is ministered to by many others. Will Shylock demand the fulfilment of the bond? Will Antonio's argosies arrive in time? Will Portia's disguise be noticed in the court? Who will choose the right casket? Will Shylock cut the flesh from Antonio?

Will he become a Christian? Will the business of the giving away of the rings ruin a happy conclusion? We may guess at some of the answers, but, if we put ourselves in the position of one seeing the play for the first time, we should realise immediately that these questions are very much in the forefront of our experience of the action. One question after another is answered—except the matter of what happens to Shylock and, importantly, they are answered without subtlety. Indeed most of them are answered with a kind of convenient adherence to the demands of the plot at any given time—it is meet that Antonio should not lose out, for example, on the general share-out of happiness at the end so, conveniently, the news comes that his enterprises are not foundered. The popularity of the play rests firmly, though not exclusively, upon these questions, and the answers that are given to them.

The question of "fallacy" demands a clear examination of aspects of the play's design. We are given no reason for Antonio's melancholy; he just is so, though it may be suggested that Shakespeare has created him thus to produce a sense of isolation which in turn will increase the *frisson* of sympathy from us in the predicament he calls upon himself. Whatever the reason, there is something unreal about the character. This quality of unreality is increased by the fact that we are continually conscious that many incidents and episodes, in themselves, have a contrived, feigned, unreal flavour. The casket episodes may be delightful but they are incredible, the bond may inject excitement into the plot, but its terms are in the realm of fantasy; the trial itself, testifying to Merchant's use of the word "fallacious" is again exciting, but, in the last analysis, incredible; the appearance of Portia in a high court, masquerading as a renowned lawyer, is an occasion for satisfying our romantic sensibilities, but it is palpably beyond the realms of possibility. And, as if to emphasise the fabulous elements in the play, the last act in Belmont, which puts aside, with complete dismissiveness, any moral compunctions about what has happened before, seems to be an idyllic haven, insulated from the harsh issues which have been enacted near the Rialto.

The creation of an unreal world through a set of incredible circumstances is reinforced by the disposition of certain scenes. The audience is lured into an aura of the fabulous by the casket episode, but it is noticeable that Shakespeare prolongs their influence by dividing it into four distinct parts. Morocco makes his debut in Act Two, scene two, and his choice in Act Two, scene seven. Arragon chooses wrongly in Act Two, scene nine and Bassanio, correctly, not until Act Three, scene two. On each occasion the fantasy quality is reinforced with delightful emphasis. Morocco's first speech to Portia after he has asked her to lead him to the caskets, has all the inconsequential bravado of a pantomime potentate:

> ... By this Symitare
> That slewe the Sophy, and a Persian Prince
> That wone three fields of Sultan Solyman,
> I would ore-stare the sternest eyes that looke:
> Out-brave the hart most daring on the earth:
> Pluck the young sucking Cubs from the she Beare,
> Yea, mock the Lyon when a rores for pray,
> To win the Lady ...
>
> [II. I. 24-31]

His reaction to the contents of the casket are in the best traditions of rhodomontade melodrama:

> Cold indeede and labour lost.
> Then farewelle heat, and welcome frost.
> [II. VII. 74-5]

Arragon, in his turn, no less reinforces the sense of delightful fable:

> I am enjoynd by oath to observe three things,
> First, never to unfold to any one
> Which casket twas I chose; next, if I faile
> Of the right casket, never in my life
> To wooe a maide in way of marriage;

Lastly,
If *I* doe faile in fortune of my choyce,
Immediately to leave you, and be gone.

[II. IX. 9-16]

These three conditions take us unequivocally into the realm of
fairy-story and enable us to take stock of the world which Portia
inhabits. A young and beautiful princess, attended only by minions,
waits for the fulfilment of an edict made by her dead father. She
is visited by two exotic potentates, but her heart is aquiver lest
one of them should open the right casket and claim her love. She
need not fear—only Prince Charming will open the right one, for
he is true in heart. All might well end very happily, except that
this particular Prince Charming has involved himself in an enter-
prise which endangers a near and dear friend. The happy ending
must be postponed until the danger is removed and its wicked
progenitor cast away.

Yet, how wicked is Shylock? It is remarkable how easy it is to
assume that Shylock's intentions, from the very beginning, are
utterly vicious—that the claiming of the flesh is inevitable from
the beginning. This is not so. In order to believe that Shylock's
intentions are, from the first, to take the matter to its inevitable
conclusion, we have, first, to deny completely the emphasis on
the fable which so much of the play makes and, second, to
overstress the implications of one particular speech of his. When
he first encounters Antonio he rails to himself about Antonio
as a fawning publican, he hates him for being a Christian, he
despises him for his attitude to usury. He say he will not forgive
him and hopes that "if I can catch him once upon the hip" he
will be happy. To catch upon the hip does not suggest killing.
It has the flavour of those threats which melodramatic villains
whisper to themselves about the hero. It is a wrestling term, and
perhaps refers to the dislocation of Jacob's hip in wrestling with
the angel. In short, Shylock will be happy to give Antonio a fall
which will be painful and humiliating.

It may be suggested that the whole of the preliminaries to the
signing of the bond are conducted by Shylock with the excited

expectation of humiliating his adversary. At this point nothing more is suggested. He and Antonio spar with each other, finding out the weak points in the duologue about Laban's sheep. The sparring over, Shylock begins the process of real humiliation. Antonio is, as it were, the challenger in the match, and Shylock speaks from his position of advantage. He taunts Antonio about how his former jibes at Jewry have now turned to requests for Jewish help:

> Fair sir, you spet on me on Wednesday last,
> You spurnd me such a day another time,
> You calld me dogge: and for these curtesies
> Ile lend you thus much moneyes.
>
> [I. III. 121-4]

Throughout this scene the atmosphere is compounded of Shylock's fierce joy in humiliating Antonio, and Antonio's grim determination to swallow the jibes for the sake of Bassanio. Up to Act Three, scene one, the motivations of Shylock are presented, albeit strongly, within the terms of the fabulous world which the casket scenes in particular have created. It is, however, in this scene that the rules of fairy-tale are broken. Jessica's departure from her father's house with his money is, in itself, of a piece with the fairy-tale atmosphere. The beleagured young maiden, tied to a mean and cruel father escapes romantically by night from his clutches into the waiting arms of her dashing young lover. If Shylock had been allowed by Shakespeare to remain in the mode of the surrounding actions of the play—that of fairy-story—the "morality" of Jessica's taking of her father's money would not arise in our minds; the villain would be merely getting his deserts. In Act Three, scene one, however, Shylock moves from one mode into another. The departure of his daughter he associates with Christian perfidy. It is, very significantly, as if a piece of his own flesh had been torn from him:

> I say my daughter is my flesh and my blood.   [III. I. 32]

It is at this point that the bond as an element in the plot acquires a more realistic significance. Immediately following upon his cry about his daughter Shylock shouts that Antonio must "look to his bond". The character has moved from agent in a fantasy into human dimensions. He begins to generate his own reactions to situations and is no longer confined within the conditioned reflexes of the fairy-tale mode. Yet, what surrounds him is still largely cast in the fairy-tale mode. After Shylock's declaration about fulfilling the bond we have, immediately, a casket scene when Bassanio makes the right choice. We are jolted back to a world of fable. This is interrupted by the news about Antonio's ships. Yet, even now, the element of happy-ever-after is strongly present. Portia's almost merry speech in which she offers money to pay Shylock has all the flavour of confidential optimism by which the pantomime princess assures her audience that, in the end, all will be well:

> When it is payd, bring your true friend along.
> My mayd *Nerissa* and my selfe meane time
> Will live as maydes and widdowes; come away,
> For you shall hence upon your wedding day.
>
> [III. II. 310-13]

Portia continues her relatively merry mood in the gamesome delight she displays, with Nerissa, at the prospect of disguising themselves. This scene induces that feeling of excitement we feel in fairy-story or pantomime when the fragile heroine leaves to take arms against the cruel monster:

> But come Ile tell thee all my whole device
> When I am in my coach, which stayes for us
> At the Park gate; and therefore hast away,
> For we must measure twenty miles to day.
>
> [III. IV. 81-4]

It is tempting to accept that George Granville's adaptation of the play first performed in 1701 and called *The Jew of Venice* was not altogether awry in concentrating itself upon the fable-quality of the plot. Significantly, Act Three, scene one (the crucial one) was omitted and Shylock's position came to be very near indeed to that of simple outrageous plot-villain. One interpolation is an entertainment in which a masque, depicting the power of love, is performed—one of the spectators is Shylock who, upon the stage-direction "Drinks", utters the following:

> I have a Mistress that out-shines 'em all—
> Commanding yours—and yours tho' the whole Sex:
> O may her charms encrease and multiply;
> My Money is my Mistress! Here's to
> Interest upon Interest.

Yet, in Shakespeare's own version, the villain escapes from the cage of the fairy-tale. By Act Three he is a wounded, dangerous, and strangely pitiable creature. He has gone beyond the simple function of being a mere melodramatic irritant to the romantic course of true love.

The most common attitude towards Jews in Elizabethan England seems to have dictated Shakespeare's outline of the character. There was no generally expressed fierce hatred of the Jews in London in the 1590s; on one occasion only did a basic and inherent attitude show itself in positive demonstration. This was during the trial of Roderigo Lopez for high treason. Lopez, a Portuguese Jew, professed Christianity like the majority of the relatively small members of his race who were in the capital. He had been physician to the Earl of Leicester and subsequently to the Queen. A claimant to the Portuguese throne arrived in London in 1692 and Lopez was alleged to have engaged in political intrigue with him. The Earl of Essex denounced him and clinched the very real charge of treason with the allegation that he had attempted to poison the Queen. His execution of 7 Jan. 1594 occasioned great and angry public excitement.

In many ways the Jew of Elizabethan imagination was a dark figure half out of fable, and his characteristics, in this context, are all present in Shylock. Cupidity, obsessive and self-indulgent thrift, meanness of spirit and a set of religious beliefs at variance with Christianity. Yet (and it is here that Shylock, in the play, steps out of his semi-mythological setting) there is much more. Shylock's attitude to usury, to the bond, are not merely stated as examples of a characteristic Jewish attitude. Shakespeare allows

Shylock some free play on our emotions. Antonio's frigid response
to Shylock's taunts:

> I am as like to call thee so againe
> To spet on thee againe, to spurne thee too.   [I. III. 125-6]

only serves to make us wonder whether he does not have some
justice in his attitude to Antonio. The defection of Jessica in
complicity with a Christian, although, as mentioned before, it is,
by itself, merely a part of the fable, becomes, when set against
Shylock's tortured grief, something to make us pause before we
condemn him outright. His plea to be granted the benefit of the
letter of the law seems, in isolation, irrationally spiteful, but,
against Portia's legal petit-point, seems no more than a demand
for the equity of an eye for an eye and a tooth for a tooth. These
factors, in themselves, cause us to wonder whether, in fact,
Shakespeare, having accepted the semi-mythological conception
of the Jew as the basis of his character (after all, he knew his box
office), bent a little backwards not so much as to avoid taking sides
as to allow his own inherent sense of fair play to manœuvre.
To put Shylock, legalistically, as he does, on a dramatic par with
Christian legality, argues for a disposition on his part to favour
Shylock. There are, however, two other factors which push
the figure of Shylock away both from the conventional idea of the
Jew and, most certainly, from the fable mode of his context.
The first is the man's pride. He has the virtue of total fidelity
(expressed without mealy-mouthed compromise) to his heritage
as a Jew; he clings to usury, not only because it is profitable but
because it is a built-in tenet of his religion. The small details of
his pride swell into largeness when he bases that pride upon
strictly human grounds: "Hath not a Jew eyes?" In the compelling
speech from which this line comes, Shakespeare opened the doors
for an audience-response which, in depth and variety, is bound
to take one's experience of the play beyond the realms of fable.

The second is in the implied reconciliation between the Christian
and the Jewish attitude. The "punishment" of Shylock is conceived,
particularly by Antonio, less as a punishment than an opportunity

for Shylock to allow himself the possibility of eternal grace by entering the Christian religion. This element in the play cannot help but arouse, except perhaps in the most rigid adherent to Christianity, the question whether the pious hope offered Shylock is a fair bargain. We have already been taught to admire Shylock's fidelity to his race and religion—now we are asked to countenance his defection from it. We are asked to watch a man being tempted to the true religion while all our emotions have convinced us that, for this man, Jewry is the only religion.

Shylock becomes too human to be accommodated within the framework of the fable. However much scholarship can point to the processes of reconciliation in this play, of, in J. R. Brown's[16] words, the many elements of the play "mingling together joyfully", it is only if we can continue to regard Shylock as a monster/comic that we can join in the dance. Portia, and Portia alone, is raised to a level which can be regarded as on a par with what Shakespeare makes of Shylock from Act Three, scene one, to his shuffling departure at the end of the trial scene. It is not without significance that the truly successful productions of this play have always depicted Shylock and Portia, in the trial scene, as equal adversaries, and mutually recognising the other as equal, they both demand, and should receive, an equal amount of sympathy and understanding from the audience. Portia represents Christian law and a spirit of reconciliation, Shylock no less, represents a Jewish interpretation of that law, and a fidelity to his own religious principles. If the tension, strung between two poles of equal strength, is maintained in the theatre, speeches like Portia's on mercy and Shylock's, which begins "what judgement . . ." ennoble the whole action. If the poles are of unequal strength, the sense of the agencies of a fable overcoming, by trickery and sententious moralising, a powerful human figure is, not to exaggerate, almost sickeningly obvious.

The play can be made, as a whole, compatible to itself in production only by allowing the strength of the fable element *and* the strength of the Shylock element full play. The result is inevitably a powerful demonstration of the singular *theatrical* effectiveness of what is *dramatically* irreconcilable.

REFERENCES

CHAPTER I

1. For information about Shakespeare's life in London see, E. K. Chambers, *William Shakespeare: a Study of Facts and Problems*, 1930; G. E. Bentley, *Shakespeare, a Biographical Handbook*, 1961; F. E. Halliday, *The Life of Shakespeare*, 1961.

2. Bentley, p. 72.

3. Quoted in J. Dover Wilson, *Life in Shakespeare's England*, 1911 (reprinted 1964), p. 231.

4. *An Elegie on the death of the famous actor Rich: Burbage, who died Marij A° 1618*; ascribed to one, Jo ffletcher.

5. Dover Wilson, p. 228.

6. *Op. cit.*, p. 173.

7. See John Dennis's epistle dedicatory to *The Comic Gallant*, 1702.

8. See M. M. Reese, *Shakespeare, his World and his Work*, 1953.

9. Ivor Brown, *How Shakespeare Spent the Day*, 1963, p. 10.

10. See Thomas Heywood, *Apologie for Actors*, 1612.

11. Quoted in *Ben Jonson*, eds Harford and Simpson, (Vol 8), 1947, p. 57.

12. There is an excellent essay on the London Theatre companies by R. A. Foakes in *Stratford-upon-Avon Studies*, III (1961).

13. For discussion of the sonnets and their dating see, J. W. Lever, *The Elizabethan Love Sonnet*, 1961; M. Seymour-Smith, *Shakespeare's Sonnets*, 1963; A. L. Rowse, *Shakespeare's Sonnets*, 1964; L. Hotson, *Mr W. H.*, 1964.

14. See E. K. Chambers, *The Disintegration of Shakespeare*, 1924; J. G. McManaway, "Recent Studies in Shakespeare's Chronology", in *Shakespeare Survey*, 3 (1950).

15. See H. R. D. Anders, *Shakespeare's Books*, 1904; K. Muir, *Shakespeare's Sources*, I, 1957.

CHAPTER 2

1. See J. Dover Wilson's Introduction to the New Cambridge edition of the play, 1939; also P. Ure (ed.) in the Arden Series, 1956, and E. A. J. Honigmann (ed.) on the problems of *King John*, Arden series, 1954.

2. The deposition of 1601 made by Augustine Phillips, one of the Lord Chamberlain's principal actors.

3. *Holinshed's Chronicle as Used in Shakespeare's Plays*, eds Allardyce Nicoll and J. Calina, 1927.

4. *Ibid.*

5. A. C. Sprague, *Shakespeare's Histories: Plays for the Stage*, 1964, p. 29.

6. Honigmann.

7. The two plays are regarded generally as having been written, successively, in late 1596 and early 1597.

8. J. Dover Wilson in his New Cambridge edition of the plays, p. xxiv.

9. See my study, "Comicall-Tragicall-Historical—A Study of Henry IVth" in *Stratford-upon-Avon Studies*, II (1961).

10. J. B. Priestley, *The English Comic Characters*, 1925 (reprinted 1963), p. 90.

11. William Empson, "Falstaff and Mr Dover Wilson", in *Kenyon Review*, 15 (1953).

12. John Wain, *The Living World of Shakespeare: a Playgoer's Guide*, 1964, p. 66.

13. *Op. cit.*, p. 65.

14. The play is usually ascribed to the period March to September 1599.

15. In his Introduction to the New Cambridge edition, p. xv.

16. A talk broadcast by Winston Churchill on 14 Jul. 1940 and published in *Into Battle*, 1941.

17. Barrett Wendell, *William Shakespeare, a Study in Elizabethan Literature*, 1894. Quoted in *A Shakespeare Encyclopaedia*, p. 334.

18. See the Introduction to the New Penguin Shakespeare edition, 1968, p. 24.

CHAPTER 3

1. See Hazlitt's *Characters of Shakespeare's Plays*, 1817.
2. Georg Brandes' *William Shakespeare*, 2 vols. 1898, contains some perspicacious comment on the play.
3. Peter Alexander, *Introductions to Shakespeare*, 1964, p. 58.
4. See Leslie Hotson, *Shakespeare versus Shallow*, 1931.
5. John Dennis, See note 7, Chapter One.
6. Jan Kott, *Shakespeare our Contemporary*, 1965, p. 72.
7. Stanley W. Wells, editor of the New Penguin edition, 1967.
8. *Op. cit.*, p. 20.

CHAPTER 4

1. From Dylan Thomas's poem, *And Death shall have no Dominion*.
2. See, for example, T. J. B. Spencer's *Elizabethan Love Stories* in the Penguin Shakespeare Library, 1976.
3. See T. J. B. Spencer's New Penguin edition of the play, 1967, p. 11.
4. No student of the play should fail to read Harley Granville Barker, *Prefaces to Shakespeare* (second series) 1927-30.
5. Spencer, p. 8.
6. One of the most moving and accomplished productions since World War II despite textual alterations and cuts.
7. The dating problem is discussed in Spencer.
8. B. Ten Brinck, *Five Lectures on Shakespeare*, 1895. Quoted in *A Shakespeare Encyclopaedia*, p. 529.
9. Brandes, quoted in *A Shakespeare Encyclopaedia*, p. 529.
10. E. E. Stoll, *Shakespeare Studies*, 1927. Quoted in *A Shakespeare Encyclopaedia*, p. 530.
11. J. Dover Wilson, *Shakespeare's Happy Comedies*, 1962.
12. See Frank Kermode, *The Mature Comedies* in *Stratford-upon-Avon Studies*, 3 (1961).
13. John Russell Brown's Introduction to the New Arden edition, 1954, is a fine study of the play.
14. John Russell Brown, *Shakespeare and his Comedies*, 1957, p. 75.
15. W. Moelwyn Merchant in his Introduction to the New Penguin edition of the play, 1967, p. 7.
16. John Russell Brown, p. 73.